Effective Leadership and Management in the Early Years

Effective Leadership and Management in the Early Years

Janet Moyles

Open University Press

Open University Press
McGraw-Hill Education
McGraw-Hill House
Shoppenhangers Road
Maidenhead
Berkshire
England
SL6 2QL

email: enquiries@openup.co.uk
world wide web: www.openup.co.uk

and Two Penn Plaza, New York, NY 10121–2289, USA

First published 2006
Reprinted 2011

A catalogue record of this book is available from the British Library

ISBN: 10: 0335 221 017 (pb) 0335 221 025 (hb)
ISBN: 13: 9780 335 221 011 (pb) 9780 335 221 028 (hb)

Library of Congress Cataloguing-in-Publication Data
CIP data applied for

Typeset by YHT Ltd, London
www.yht.ltd.uk
Printed in the UK by Ashford Colour Press Ltd, Gosport, Hampshire

Contents

Charts

Acknowledgements

There were many people involved in the creation of the original ELMES (EY) materials. Particular thanks go to Richard Yates for his outstanding work on the research element of the project and much of the report writing up. Special thanks also go to Maxine Levy who worked tirelessly on keeping those involved in the project informed and supported, and to Douglas Stuart who added his invaluable knowledge from time to time.

The European Social Fund, Essex County Council and Southend Borough Council all contributed financial support to the project, without which it would never have happened. Particular thanks go to Aimi MacCormac, Julie Bravery and Diana Batemen for their confidence in the outcomes. Anglia Ruskin University also provided support for the project, as did Cambridgeshire local education authority.

Dr Siân Adams and Helen Broomby served as consultants to the project and brought extremely valuable knowledge of early years leadership and management to bear on the ongoing progress and ultimate findings of the research. In the latter stages of the writing of this book, Jillian Rodd and Liz Brooker offered very useful commentary and advice which was welcome.

After an initial trawl of the (limited) literature on early years leadership and management and delving more deeply into overall leadership and management theories, the continuous involvement of a number of practising leaders and managers was invaluable in ensuring that the final version of ELMS was accessible and comprehensible to all those leading and managing the full range of early years settings. In alphabetical order they were: Amber Abbs, Diane Allmark, Ann Barker, Jackie Deacon, Kay Dimelow, Catherine House, Sally Rodricks, Annie Tann, Jenny Woodford and Angie Wright.

Introduction

About ELMS – the Effective Leadership and Management Scheme for the Early Years

There has been an unprecedented focus recently on the early years of children's lives and the impact of the various adults who work and play with children in the birth to 5–6 years age range. Staff in early years settings have had to adapt to many changes and demands from local authorities and national government, none more so than those who suddenly found themselves in a leadership and management role in increasingly complex small early years businesses and settings often without formal training or qualifications. For example, consider the playgroup leader, a mother of young children, who suddenly found herself responsible for, amongst other things, sums of government money for 3- and 4-year-olds, accountability for paperwork returns in relation to these children, having to justify the educational experiences provided for these children, and ensuring that staff within the setting received opportunities for professional development. In addition, competition from other providers in the area meant that she also needed to learn how to market the setting to its best possible advantage and learn to communicate effectively with parents in a new leadership capacity and also to work in partnership with a new managing body.

Until recently, little training was offered to those who lead and manage early years settings, and it is credit to all involved that many of these people have worked really hard to enhance their own skills with whatever resources (albeit limited) were available at the time, often against a raft of pressures. As Ebbeck and Waninganayake (2002) suggest, 'there are few publicly acknowledged leaders and no set of common expectations for leaders in early childhood'. Yet there is significant evidence from several research and theoretical sources to suggest that the quality of a setting can depend heavily upon the quality, skills and effectiveness of those in charge. For example, Solley (2003), in a paper given at the Institute of Education, asserted that enthusiasm, passion, inspiration and advocacy rate as the great strengths of a leader. In the Effective Provision of Pre-School Education project (Sylva *et al.* 2004), it was found that the higher the qualifications of managers, the higher the quality of children's curriculum experiences, the more effective the programme structure and the better the relations with, and between, staff and parents (Taggart *et al.* 2000). The importance of leaders and managers cannot be underestimated.

The Effective Leadership and Management Scheme (ELMS) is just what the title suggests – a tool for all those who lead and manage early years settings which they can use for evaluating their effectiveness in the role of leader/manager. Its purpose is to ensure that children and practitioners in those settings receive the best possible experiences and direction in their work and play and that parents and carers can have confidence in the particular setting attended by their children.

The development of ELMS involved a range of leaders and managers working alongside researchers and consultants to investigate together the components of effective early years leadership and management. This resultant publication is unique not only in providing a thorough analysis of the leader's/manager's role and presenting it as a typology, but also in offering a clear, in-depth view of that role through a systematic review of the literature and consultation with experts. It also presents ways in which the leader/manager can undertake self-evaluation or work alongside a peer to understand their own strengths and challenges more readily. Such a typology offers a framework which classifies features and components of the leaders'/managers' roles. As Rodd (2006: 52) suggests: 'A typology is a means of, or framework for, classifying selected factors or features. It can be used as a summary or protocol for understanding the structure of a phenomenon ... one advantage of a typology of leadership is that aspiring and formal leaders are alerted to significant features of effective leadership, thus avoiding a trial and error approach to learning how to be an effective leader.' This is certainly the intention with ELMS.

So what are leadership and management? What research led to the development of ELMS? Who was involved in formulating it? How much confidence can users have in its integrity and reliability? Chapter 1 sets out to answer these questions and to establish the context for leaders/managers to understand and utilize the evaluation scale. It outlines how the overall content of ELMS was established and explains briefly the layout and presentation. Chapter 2 outlines how ELMS is used to evaluate the early years head's leadership and management role and a potential grading system for such evaluation. The following chapters then expand on the main components of the typology, exemplified with appropriate scenarios and stories of real-life situations. The final chapter explores the various purposes and uses of ELMS and also draws together the different elements and makes links with other training opportunities for leaders/managers, including giving some specific annotated references for follow-up reading.

First, however, we need to look at the terms 'leadership' and 'management' which, up to this point, have been used as if they were interchangeable.

Leadership or management?

Concepts of leadership and management are not yet fully explored in early years terms. In fact, in the early years we still have a problem with what to call our setting's leaders/ managers. In schools, it's easy: headteachers. But it could be argued that this term is insufficient to describe and define the role undertaken by, for example, those who head up children's centres, where the job is both more multi-dimensional and multi-professional. Perhaps we need to adopt a new title in early years – 'head' or perhaps 'EC principal' – so that the complexities of the role are subsumed within the title. To save clumsiness in this publication, those leading and managing settings will, from this point onwards, mainly be called 'heads' with specific terms used where they are appropriate.

The role of an early years setting head is currently not well researched. Muijs *et al.* (2004) carried out an in-depth review of the literature into early childhood leadership and identified a paucity of research, despite a high potential for leadership activity in the field. They conclude that there is a clear need to identify what is effective leadership practice in terms of processes and outcomes within early childhood and call for theoretically based studies that allow different models and characteristics to be empirically tested, deeming these to be long overdue. They also highlight the serious lack of leadership training which could mean that many early childhood leaders are significantly under-prepared for their role – a fact substantiated by our research and by the participating heads and consultants.

ELMS had to draw extensively on leadership and management texts and educational research (of which there's been a plethora over the past two decades) because of this paucity. These are useful but do not offer the full picture for early years leadership and management because of their focus on statutory schooling practices, so adjustment is always needed in translating these studies into early childhood terms. Additionally, the concept of leadership, in particular, is complex and has undergone a number of metamorphoses over the past two decades (see Grace 1995). It is Fink's view (2005: xiv) that 'we are making the business of leadership so complicated that we seem to need "super-heroes"'. Later he goes on to say about good heads he has met that 'They are not heroes. ... Rather they are ordinary people who through extraordinary commitment, effort and determination have become extraordinary, and have made the people around them exceptional' (p. xviii). This appealed to us in the development of ELMS because, in working with our focus group, we increasingly recognized that these early years heads were extraordinary people, in some cases not nearly well enough acknowledged either financially or professionally for the skills and understanding they possess.

Currently, 'leadership' is the favoured term in signifying the headteacher's role. Leadership embraces a number of other concepts, and Fink (2005: xvi) suggests that leaders should be 'leaders of learning' first and foremost, which involves all of the following: understanding learning, critical thinking, contextual understanding, political acumen, emotional understanding, making connections and futures thinking. (This is just one example of how an educational focus alone does not meet early childhood leadership needs in relation, for example, to care, although other aspects certainly need to be included in the early years head's role.) At the same time, Fink emphasizes that 'leadership is a very personal thing, and one's view of leadership reflects "who" you are, "what" you are, and "where" you are in space and time' (p. xiv). This appears to be much nearer to what we might expect in early childhood. It suggests that trying to develop any overall typology is extremely difficult but the research focus group decided that the typology in use would enable these personalizing elements to be included.

Other writers have offered different views. For example, 'leadership is less a specific set of behaviours than it is creating an environment in which people are motivated to produce and move in the direction of the leader' (Horner 2003: 30). Harris and Lambert (2003: 167) suggests that 'Leadership is essentially the process of building and maintaining a sense of vision, culture and interpersonal relationships'. Oldroyd *et al.* (1996) offer a definition of leader as a person who exercises power, authority and influence over a group derived from his/her acceptance by the group and his/her position within the formal organization, whereas Jackson (2003: xvi) asserts that 'The role of the "leader" ... is to harness, focus, liberate, empower and align ... leadership towards common purposes'. Jackson goes on to say that 'Leadership, as we have come to understand it, does not exist in a literal sense. It is an enacted variable, dependent upon interactions between leader, follower and context' (p. xvi).

Collins (2001: 20) offers a five-level hierarchy of leadership where level 4 is the effective leader who 'catalyzes commitment to and vigorous pursuit of a clear and compelling vision, stimulating higher performance standards': something we would certainly wish to aim for in early childhood. Heifetz and Linsky (2002: 3) emphasize that leadership is about 'getting more out of life by putting more into it' and 'putting yourself and your ideas on the line, responding effectively to the risks, and living to celebrate your many efforts'. Day (2004) feels that the most successful leaders are those who have a deep-seated passion for students, school and community; again something very much on a par with early years practitioners' and heads' thinking (see Moyles 2001).

Added to these views is the gender dimension. Most leaders in early childhood are female and, according to Shakeshaft (1989: 12) there is a 'female culture' of leadership with distinct characteristics, such as greater interpersonal care and sensitivities than those shown by men, a strong and central focus on the quality both of teaching and learning and of relationships with children, and a more democratic and participatory style of decision making, with different conceptions of relations with the wider community, of the use of power and of the nature of educational leadership. For example, Whalley (1999) suggests that women favour influence rather than authority in undertaking a leadership role. Whilst these views have changed somewhat in recent times, with male leaders being encouraged perhaps towards these 'feminine' attributes, leadership roles in early years are still relatively new and these factors still need to be considered in this evolving field. Rodd (2006: 50) argues that

> Leadership is often described in terms of the relationships built up by the leader and team members. The quality of relationships tends to be evaluated in terms of attributes such as empathy, warmth, respect and genuineness – all of which are associated more with the feminine stereotype. Although men and women who are leaders display both masculine and feminine traits and behaviours, the traditional features of the female approach . . . [are] argued to be more appropriate and successful . . . in early childhood settings.

Lipman-Blumen (1992: 1) suggests that 'female leadership is no longer an oxymoron. Viewed from the perspective of global interdependence, it contains the seeds of connective leadership, a new, integrative model of leadership more suited to the dramatically changing workplace of the twenty-first century'. Certainly, integrative and connective models are vital in early childhood education and care, for they are the basis of the ways in which practitioners work with children and families.

What is clear in all these attempts at describing and defining the role of leader and the task of leadership is that current thinking is moving in the direction of writing about 'leadership' throughout organizations rather than focusing on the 'leader' (Bennett *et al.* 2003). Whilst leadership theory reflects significant diversity and richness, it also appears to be something of an elusive concept and a deeply complex subject: as Bennett *et al.* (2003: ix) also suggest, 'leadership is a contested concept'. Some writers have identified skills such as establishing the culture of the organization, empowering others, articulating vision and exhibiting strategic thinking, whilst yet others view leadership as much more difficult to pin down to such specifics. However, without such 'pinning down' it would be impossible to offer any kind of guidance such as ELMS and would leave early years heads in the position of having little clear understanding of the components of their role.

The term 'management' is no less complex, although some writers suggest that it is a more observable behaviour than leadership. As Crawford (2003: 63–4) advises: 'management brings order and consistency to key dimensions of an organisation. Leadership is about coping with change . . . educational management and effective leadership are symbiotic'. He goes on to say: 'Understanding the importance of the complementarity of the leadership and management functions helps us to understand why people with very different personalities can be equally effective' (p. 71). Grace (1995: 192) insists that 'management is about achieving organisational effectiveness', whereas Collins (2001), in his five-level hierarchy, sees level 3 as a competent manager who 'organizes people and resources towards the effective and efficient pursuit of predetermined objectives' (p. 2). O'Sullivan (2003: 5) states that 'Management is a combination of theory and practice that is designed to ensure that the work of an organisation is developed, supported and guided by an individual or team so as to effectively meet the organisation's purposes'. This is supported by Harris and Lambert (2003: 167) who believe that management 'is the co-ordination, support and monitoring of organisational activities'. It seems, as Mintzberg (2004: 141) suggests, that 'Management has to be *everywhere*. It has to flow with the activity'. Trying to incorporate all these ideas into ELMS was no mean feat. It can be seen that not only are both leadership and management complex concepts but there is major overlap in their contents as well.

Having looked at these basic concepts in a range of leadership and management literature, what seems clear is that, in general, management involves control, direction, problem solving, planning, monitoring, resourcing, negotiating and doing, whereas leadership involves insight, vision, capacity to change, wisdom, commitment, liaison and communication skills. At its extreme, some writers seem to believe that management is (at least historically) about control, whereas leadership is more about democracy. In early childhood terms, there are still elements of both to be seen in practice and this must be reflected in typologies such as ELMS.

One of the few distinct early years leadership and management texts is that of Smith and Langston (1999). They define a manager as someone who controls, does, organizes, accepts current practices, administrates, follows through, co-ordinates and is motivated by discipline. On the other hand, they feel that a leader inspires, thinks, motivates, initiates change, has vision, dictates, takes decisions, sets objectives, sets the pace, inspires loyalty and is self-sufficient. They see both leadership and management as being vital elements in running an early years setting and offer a useful, if long, explanation which we have essentially adopted in ELMS:

> Leadership and management complement each other. . . . Where they differ is with regard to change. Managers cope with the complexities and results of change while leaders inspire and initiate change. Both characteristics are important in the context of change within education, particularly at the pre-school stage, where the parent/client teacher/manager relationship is altering rapidly. In order for early years establishments to achieve the high standards expected of them they must attract people who are capable of motivating others towards attainable goals: in short they must inspire loyalty and act as a driving force. The same person, however, needs to establish procedures for staff and make a rational and balanced assessment of current situations; she or he needs to be able to plan, to organise, to forecast and to control so that visions are turned into reality. As well as being a leader and a manager, the same person needs to be an efficient administrator who checks the tasks, procedures and resources within the organisation. The sort of person who can successfully lead others needs to combine all three elements – leader, manager, administrator – no mean feat and a little like spinning plates! The leader initiates the ideas and puts them into practice. The manager keeps them going and organises their progress. The administrator makes sure they are achievable.
>
> (Smith and Langston 1999: 6–7)

This mirrors McEwan's (2003) seven steps to becoming an effective leader:

1. Establish, implement and achieve academic standards.
2. Be an instructional resource for your staff.
3. Create a school culture and climate conducive to learning (for everyone).
4. Communicate the vision and mission of your school.
5. Set high expectations of your staff and yourself.
6. Develop teacher leaders.
7. Establish and maintain positive relationships with children, staff and parents.

The element of administration seems to be relatively unique to Smith and Langston and perhaps would normally be subsumed within the management role in wider leadership and management literature. Certainly, for ELMS we made the decision to focus on leadership and management in the terms already outlined above. Oldroyd *et al.* (1996) include leader, manager and administrator in their definitions, but Gold and Evans (1998: 26) suggest that 'Within these definitions, it seems that management and leadership overlap . . . but leadership has an almost spiritual dimension, paying more attention to beliefs and values'.

Rodd (2006: 20), drawing on the work of Law and Glover (2000), proffers a useful set of differences between leaders and managers (see Table I.1).

Table I.1 Managers vs leaders

Managers . . .	Leaders . . .
• *Plan*: set objectives, forecast, analyse problems, make decisions, formulate policy • *Organize*: determine what activities are required to meet objectives, classify work, divide it up and assign it • *Co-ordinate*: inspire staff to contribute both individually and as a group to the organization's objectives • *Control*: check performance against plans, develop people and maximize their potential to achieve agreed outcomes	• *Give direction*: find a way forward, communicate a clear direction, identify new goals, services and structures • *Offer inspiration*: have ideas and articulate thoughts that motivate others • *Build teamwork*: use teams as the most effective form of leadership, spending their time building and encouraging collaboration • *Set an example*: model what leaders do and how they do it • *Gain acceptance*: act in ways that engender acknowledgement of their leadership status in followers

Source: Rodd (2006: 20)

Bennett *et al.* (2003 : x) sum up our feelings in attempting to develop ELMS from this diverse, and sometimes contradictory background to understanding leadership and management:

> whichever of these broad understandings of leadership [and management] you adopt has profound implications for how you define or identify 'good' or 'effective' leadership and the kinds of skills or capacities that you identify as necessary.

We attempted to use as broad a base as possible to reflect the many different kinds of components, styles and approaches to leadership and management that we were likely to see in the plethora of early years settings, for example children's centres, pre-schools, independent nurseries, Foundation Stage settings. At times, then, leadership and management 'purists' may consider that we have not kept strictly to all the background knowledge and understanding about the concepts. However, we also had our willing group of heads of early years settings and our consultants who added their own dimensions to our practical and theoretical exploration of the issues. It was these people who determined the final content and presentation of ELMS. In the next chapter we explore other issues related to the development of the typology.

1 Background research and how ELMS evolved

The origin of ELMS is located in an extension of several years of research into early years practices by the author, in particular *Statements of Entitlement to Play* (StEPs: Moyles and Adams 2001), the *Study of Pedagogical Effectiveness in Early Learning* (SPEEL: Moyles *et al.* 2002), the *Essex Effective Pedagogy Evaluation Scheme* (EEPES (EY): Moyles and Musgrove 2003) and *Inside the Foundation Stage* (Adams *et al.* 2004).

StEPs explored with early years practitioners their roles in providing playful learning experiences for young children and analysed in some depth the challenges and dilemmas facing early years workers. SPEEL was undertaken for the Department for Education and Skills (DfES) and concentrated on identifying attributes of effectiveness of early years practitioners. EEPES (EY) was commissioned by Essex County Council and Essex Early Years Development and Childcare Partnership (EYDCP) and culminated in the development of an evaluation scheme to assess (and explain) effective early years pedagogy. The *Inside the Foundation Stage* project was funded by the Association of Teachers and Lecturers (ATL) and aimed to analyse the effects of the introduction of the Foundation Stage and its curriculum guidance on the quality of the curriculum experiences provided by practitioners for 4- and 5-year-old children. All of these projects showed that quality practices for children relied heavily on the quality of the practitioners and also upon the quality of the leadership and management systems operating in the various settings. Effective heads are known to enable practitioners to develop the effectiveness of their practices and thus to benefit children and their families (Daly *et al.* 2004; Sadek and Sadek 2004).

Other studies have equally shown the necessity for highly skilled and well-qualified leaders and managers (see, for example, Rodd 1998, 2006; Taggart *et al.* 2000; Aubrey *et al.* 2005). The development and rolling out across the country of the National Professional Qualification for Integrated Centre Leaders (NPQICL: National College for School Leadership/Pen Green Centre 2005) is also evidence of the importance now placed by policy makers on the training of early years leaders/managers. ELMS, as we shall see, can offer guidance and support for any other scheme or leadership training, as well as being used on its own by individuals or peer groups, enabling them to evaluate their own skills, knowledge and understanding. But first we need to look at how ELMS was developed, who and what was involved and how we established the validity of the final document. The final part of the chapter outlines the basic conceptualization of ELMS as a tree.

Who and what was involved in the development of ELMS?

Like most research, ELMS depended on acquiring funding, in this case from three sources: the European Social Fund (ESF), Essex County Council and Southend Borough Council. One of the focuses at that time for ESF funding was related to provision of support for women managing small, independent businesses: both authorities were also becoming interested in early years leadership and agreed to provide additional funding. Cambridgeshire also agreed to participate 'in kind' and to identify settings with effective leaders who might be involved in the research. Thus this enabled the researchers to focus on private and voluntary, maintained and non-maintained settings in three different authorities in the eastern region of England.

To begin the process of identifying the qualities, skills, attributes, characteristics and attitudes of the effective early years leader and manager, we needed to establish just how much, if any, research and literature existed about early years leadership and management. The project therefore commenced with a broad literature review which continued throughout the duration of ELMS development – and beyond. The subject of the initial review was 'What are the components of effective early years leadership and management?' Researchers began trawling for relevant literature, including seminal publications on business leadership and organizational theory as well as material specific to the early years. Book sources, websites and electronic databases were all used. This extensive literature review revealed that, whilst many studies have emphasized the importance of highly qualified and skilled leaders/managers as a result of examining children's and practitioners' experiences, there has been little definitive work on what makes for effective early years leadership and management. We were able (in the early stages) to identify only three dedicated books – Lyus (1998), Rodd (1998) and Smith and Langston (1999) – which were used extensively to support the research. Jillian Rodd's book (updated in 2006), in particular, offered a number of central insights and readers will find that her book is quite heavily referenced in ELMS. Isles-Buck and Newstead (2003), O'Sullivan (2003) and Sadek and Sadek (2004) also provided useful further information and ideas during the write-up of the research.

The initial sifting through of these and other leadership and management texts (see Introduction and References) enabled the development of an original listing of attributes under the following headings:

- Leadership qualities
- Management skills
- Professional attributes
- Personal characteristics and attitudes.

From the beginning, the project employed two consultants both of whom had extensive knowledge, experience and understanding of leading and managing early years settings. In order to ensure that the listing would make sense to a focus group of early years heads, these two consultants examined and challenged the lists, and undertook such tasks as adapting the wording to make it more accessible and useable. That done, it was time to turn the lists over to practising heads of settings, sixteen of whom had been identified within the authorities involved. These sixteen, plus the two consultants, became our focus group and, from this point on, worked towards the development of the final typology in relation to their own leadership and management roles, gradually taking over ownership of its content, presentation and application.

The focus group's main brief was to

- support the development of the overall content of ELMS and validate its contents;
- help us to produce exemplification materials for ELMS (including cameos and other stories);
- support the production of ELMS in terms of establishing a suitable layout and presentation.

To these ends they undertook a number of activities, one of which included keeping a diary for just a week in which they jotted down common basic events and daily tasks within their roles. The diaries offered the research team an accurate and current portrait of the daily lives of the heads, an enriching experience for the researchers who read the completed diaries. Initially, the focus group were asked to list the many components of their role, which produced the following enlightening list. This list, culled from these diaries, is neither ranked nor weighted. It should be emphasized that members of the focus group recorded one week only of their roles. Needless to say, if the exercise had been undertaken over a longer period, the list, already abridged, would have been considerably more extensive.

Some of the tasks of a 'typical' leader or manager

- Arrange daily activities and classrooms
- Type up and record daily activities
- Brief others on daily activities
- Socialize with staff and listen to staff's ideas
- Answer and make telephone calls
- Read and organize post
- Undertake any pending administration
- Ensure staff numbers each day and contact supply staff
- Liaise with governors, officials and other managers
- Organize elections for new post for governor and teacher
- Discuss budget with financial adviser
- Undertake other finance/budget-related tasks
- Meet current and prospective children and parents
- Teach children
- Visit classrooms to check on special needs children
- Monitor others teaching children
- Organize and attend assemblies and gatherings
- Take relevant measures concerning injured child
- Assess children in relation to the Foundation Stage profile
- Undertake individual educational plans and liaise with SENCO about SEN children
- Deal with naughty children
- Listen to complaints and concerns from parents and staff
- Organize and make coffee and lunch
- Mark homework and give feedback
- Complete outstanding work in the evenings
- Update staff handbook and other documents
- Read research publications
- Read DfES documents such as *Every Child Matters*
- Read OfSTED documents and prepare for inspection
- Write school/child/annual reports and proofread others
- Delegate tasks in relation to inspection and monitoring
- Organize and attend open evening
- Attend professional development session
- Ensure the hygiene of food and snacks
- Organize professional catering for upcoming event
- Organize maintenance work during holidays
- Organize and welcome visiting children, parents and students
- Show guests around the setting
- Settle in students
- Talk to parent group about reading and phonics
- Organize school trips
- Visit Beacon schools and liaise with fellow professionals
- Communicate formally and informally with parents
- Undertake staff appraisals
- Organize the setting's website

- Respond to e-mail requests
- Organize training courses
- Organize library and play resources
- Liaise with health visitors over 'at risk children'
- Read commercial publications such as *Nursery World* and *Early Years Educator*
- Organize and order resources such as books and art equipment
- Organize class photos and website photos
- Organize displays and wall mounts
- Plan essentials for the coming week
- Organize and run staff meetings
- Meet and maintain communication with EYDCP representatives
- Meet and maintain communication with LEA representatives
- Organize and attend health and safety meetings
- Organize and attend local nursery group meetings
- Organize and attend senior management meetings
- Attend heads' meeting and liaise with other heads
- Clear up and organize the kitchen
- Buy cards and presents for birthdays and professional thank you gestures
- Discuss leadership and management styles with staff
- Finalize and present 'staff awards'.

This list brings to mind the remarks of Fink (2005) in the Introduction, about heads needing to be 'super-heroes'.

All omissions, repetitions, misplaced or missed emphases in the original ELMS document, were noted and changed as a result of the diaries. It was also interesting to compare the list above with the developing leadership and management typology from the literature reviews and to note that, structurally, the evolving ELMS typology underwent only minimal change for all these factors to be taken into account. What it did show us at this stage was how diverse and complex the head's leadership and management role actually is, confirming for us the need to establish common ground on which all early years heads would be able to consider their roles and deepen their knowledge of everyday practices. One of the challenges is to enable users of such a typology to 'see' their everyday role with different eyes: it is undeniably difficult in the busyness of day-to-day practice to understand properly the countless activities that an individual undertakes. One benefit of the list above is that it begins to show individuals the extent of their roles – and there are only 24 hours in any day!

At each of our monthly meetings, different aspects of the typology were explored directly in relation to the heads' day-to-day practices. We delved into their attitudes and feelings towards their work and into their concepts of such aspects as vision, charisma, risk taking, humour and motivation. How was it possible to 'classify' these aspects in some way? How could they possibly be written down in such a way that they sounded as important as they clearly are? Once the draft typology was available, heads were asked to try to 'behaviourize' the skills and attributes identified as contributing to effective leadership and management.

Whilst developing EEPES (EY), the research team had been successful in identifying aspects of effective pedagogy and then making each one measurable by finding specific behaviours associated with it which could be ranked. For example, the entry 'Enables children's choice of learning' could be expressed and explained by statements such as 'Helps children to make choices from the range of available activities and resources' (Acceptable level), 'Involves children in planning their own choice of activities over a given period of time' and 'Monitors children's choice of activities and uses this to inform planning for child-initiated activities' (Good level), and 'Teaches children how to reflect upon their activities and experiences and to use this in making choices about suitable follow-on ac-tivities. Plans learning activities in collaboration with children' (Very good level) (Moyles and Musgrove 2003: 30). This proved to be exceptionally difficult in ELMS, particularly in relation to leadership, thus supporting much of the thinking behind the literature outlined in the Introduction – that leadership is related to vision and other relatively intangible concepts, whereas management is more about putting structures into place to ensure that intentions happen. It seemed easier to turn management attributes into behaviours rather than leadership aspects.

Particular qualities, such as charisma and sense of humour, were not capable of being classified or behaviourized. The researchers did not want to fall into the trap of 'MacNa-mara's Fallacy' (Handy 1989): that is, making what is measurable important rather than what is important measurable. A way of 'grading' the components was vital if the final document was to be useful to heads and potential evaluators – grading would enable an identification of strengths and weaknesses which is important in encouraging heads to use the typology and to be honest about themselves in that role and in that setting. The focus group decided that the best kind of grading system would be one undertaken through a series of reflective questions (see Chapter 2). The 'grades' that feature in ELMS are (im-portantly) guidelines to be used at the evaluator's discretion. These are explained in the following chapter. Now a brief explanation of the validity and reliability of the ELMS ty-pology is outlined.

How much confidence can users have in the integrity and reliability of ELMS?

The ELMS document went through several transformations before the focus group and researchers were satisfied that we had covered as many of the main aspects of the early years head's role as were relevant without being overwhelming. Each statement was written, rewritten, amended, torn apart and revised several times during group meetings and in the interim periods through post and e-mail. The resultant document is capable of use by leaders and managers working in a wide range of settings with children from birth to 6 years of age. (As many of the skills are generic, it may well be that ELMS has uses with a wider age range but this has not been validated.)

The researchers wanted to ensure that the outcome of the project had three types of validity: content, construct and face validity. As our initial research was both comprehen-sive and systematic, and drew on the expertise of numerous early years specialists as well as physical resources, content validity seemed assured. Face validity was established by prac-titioners in the field recognizing the typology as accurately reflecting their work. It was also essential to establish whether the constructs (the contents and the concepts behind them) would also stand up to scrutiny. As well as focus group meetings, numerous other methods were undertaken to ensure a high level of content and construct validity.

The literature plus the input of the consultants enabled the first content draft to be produced. The product of this was an inventory of early years skills – a typology of qualities, skills, attributes, characteristics and attitudes (some essential, some desirable) required for effective early years leadership and management.

Continuing to organize the material as a list or typology of components needed for effective leadership and management was the most realistic way to begin construction of the evaluation scheme. The involvement of many experts, that is to say those either doing the job or supporting it, meant that, from the start, we were confident that ELMS had both face and construct validity.

Researchers, heads, and early years consultants felt that the more difficult, immeasurable and abstract sections of ELMS needed extended explanation. Cameos serve this purpose and contextualize some of the sections, placing them firmly within an early years setting. As Adams (2005: 220) suggests, 'practitioners do not readily identify and articulate their values and beliefs. ... In order to help them locate their own voices, to articulate pedagogical values and beliefs, they need opportunities and time to recount the anecdotes and stories of the daily activities in which they are engaged.' Certainly, our heads were given this opportunity and the second group who trialled the materials appreciated these stories of real leadership experiences. Comments such as: 'These stories really bring all the detail to life' and 'I know just how that person felt – I worked for a head just like that', gave us confidence that we should use such stories, albeit selectively, in the final document.

The number and content of the cameos was determined through consultation with everyone involved and merged the real-life opinions and experiences of heads with up-to-the-minute research and management theory. The focus group members were asked to name the twelve or so most 'awkward' sections of ELMS, the ones 'in need of further explanation'. These were then tallied, so the final version of ELMS reflects the consensus of opinion as to the level of difficulty of different items.

Reliability was much more difficult to establish. It required that we were able to trial ELMS over time – which was something we could not do in the timescale of the research. It would have been useful to have used ELMS with our sixteen focus group heads consistently over time and then been able to report on the reliability of the typology in identifying effective leadership and management practices. As a measure of ELMS's effectiveness, each of our sixteen heads selected sixteen other willing volunteers in similar roles with whom to work through the final document. The purpose was for them to use ELMS and see whether it was possible to achieve outcomes similar to those established when they used ELMS on themselves. The new focus group reported the final ELMS document comprehensive, useable and effective in enabling them to identify their strengths and challenges and to consider their future training needs. The content has since been used successfully by two authorities in their own training sessions.

The meaning of ELMS and the metaphor of a tree

Whilst Fink (2005) suggests the metaphor of a spider's web as epitomizing the spread and interconnectedness of leadership and management, we felt that this was a rather fragile concept for something so robust. After much discussion, the focus group felt that ELMS was best conceptualized as a tree – the ELM. Like a tree, early years leadership and management fans out. It involves having certain qualities, skills, attributes, characteristics and attitudes, within which are embedded more qualities, skills, attributes, characteristics and attitudes ... and so on. Indeed, the tree, with its associations of branching and growth, and strength and reliability, is, we feel, a suitable metaphor for ELMS.

The ELMS tree is composed of four main sections called 'branches'. The branches represent:

1. Leadership qualities
2. Management skills
3. Professional skills and attributes
4. Personal characteristics and attitudes.

These four branches were identified through the research as being the key areas that constitute effective early years leadership and management. They encompass all the essential components necessary for effective leadership and management which appear within at least one of the branches. However, it is worth pointing out now that there is some necessary and unavoidable overlap in many of these aspects: as we discovered in exploring the leadership and management literature in the Introduction. The concepts of leadership and management in themselves are not discrete and neither are the many aspects which make up the overall dimensions of the role. Sometimes the differences are quite subtle, for example, different forms of communication across different circumstances are included in both the Management Skills branch and the Professional Skills and Attributes branch.

On the branches are subsections called 'stems': these are the embedded qualities, skills, attributes, characteristics and attitudes that grow out of the four main branches. As examples, under the main branch 'Leadership Qualities', the first stem (1.1) is 'Be visionary', the fifth stem (1.5) is 'Be flexible and versatile'. Under the main branch 'Personal Characteristics and Attitudes', the first stem (4.1) is 'Have knowledge of, and a natural enthusiasm for, children, teaching and learning', the fourth stem (4.4) is 'Have a continued commitment to and vested interest in children's overall development'.

Each stem has further subsections called 'leaves'. These reflect more defined, precise qualities, skills, attributes, characteristics and attitudes required of effective leaders and managers. Examples from Stem 4.1 are: 4.1a 'Understand and value the dual responsibility of early years providers to care, to ensure learning and to teach', and 4.1b 'Understand the concept of "in loco parentis"'. Evaluation is undertaken mainly through close scrutiny of the contents of the leaves alongside a series of questions.

The full content of branches, stems and leaves is laid out in detail in the ELMS tree typology which appears at the end of Chapter 2. Also in Chapter 2, the use of ELMS for evaluation purposes is outlined and discussed, including the potential purposes for such evaluation. The evaluation questions are also explored and explained.

2 ELMS as typology and an evaluation tool

The purpose of this chapter is to outline how ELMS has been formulated to evaluate the early years head's leadership and management role and a potential grading system for such evaluation. The final pages of the chapter set out the detailed Index of ELMS's stems, branches and leaves.

Of all the challenges that faced us during the development of ELMS, finding a way for users to 'rate' or evaluate themselves was perhaps the most difficult. Yet, in some ways, it is the most important because if one understands where one 'is' currently, then one can also consider what training and professional development opportunities are going to be most beneficial. ELMS needed to accomplish the dual purpose firstly, of identifying the level of operation of the user and, secondly, of actually starting (or promoting) this process of professional development.

Numerous attempts were made by researchers, practitioners and early years consultants to define the components using lists of behaviours and physical actions. For example, stem 1.1 (Be visionary) might look something like: 'The leader/manager makes time to sit and consider the future of the setting for, say, twenty minutes each day. The leader/manager provides all staff with an updated mission statement half-yearly/annually'. As is clear from this, defining each component of ELMS could have had a negative rather than a positive impact. We were also concerned that it could be limiting and create false realities.

There was a further dilemma: in behaviourizing ELMS, more information would have been needed. Clearly, whilst each component is currently 'subjective', if each had been elaborated further – even in the name of being more 'objective' – the document would have been unacceptably long. Our focus group were adamant that the length as it currently appears was about right to still be useable and useful – any more would definitely have been too much.

The researchers believe – and there is ample evidence from others, for example Mailhos (1999), Reynolds (1999), Muijs and David (2001) – that personal and professional development is the product of reflection and self-awareness. Self-identity cannot be taken as a given but has to be achieved and sustained by the process of reflection. Because of this, we felt it was necessary to provide a scheme that would encourage users to analyse their current thinking, approaches and capabilities and to deliberate on each component. In this way, the user would discover what underpins each branch, stem and leaf in the context of the unique, individual setting. Users of ELMS determine for themselves whether or not they satisfy each component and decide to what extent each one reflects their current qualities, skills, attributes, characteristics and attitudes. This may sound idiosyncratic and, for this reason, we would encourage users to undertake peer evaluation, or at least to share their self-evaluation with a trusted colleague. If, for example, the evaluation is used as a pre-inspection check, then there is no point in not being honest with oneself about one's strengths, weaknesses and challenges. These might be all too quickly identified anyway.

It is fair to say that a great deal of reflection is involved in the process of self-evaluation (see, for example, Ghaye and Ghaye 1998; Gold and Evans 1998; Yorke-Barr 2001). Reflecting on one's role and on policy and practice is the same as reflecting on anything else in our lives: it is about thinking deeply and contemplating how things 'are'. In reflecting in depth, people also analyse whether everything is as it should be or whether changes are needed. We have coined the phrase 'active reflection', because we feel it is important that everyone considers her/his life carefully, analysing, evaluating and interpreting not only what 'is' but also how things should or could be different. Reflection also operates at the level of surfacing one's own beliefs and values. As Johnson (1999: 37) suggests:

> Our beliefs shape our actions. They either limit our scope for action or they empower us to develop positively in new directions. ... [I]t is important to develop greater self-awareness and understanding of these areas of your life in work where limiting beliefs are holding you back and preventing you from realizing your full potential.

Active reflection enables leaders and managers to discover, rediscover and understand the complex range of knowledge, skills and understanding they have and to develop and use the intellectual and emotional power within themselves to try to improve or enhance their situation (Fullan 2003; Day 2005). From their research and conceptualization of the issues, Ghaye and Ghaye (1998) also suggest that reflection has the potential to empower individuals, because the process enables them to become more effective, personally and professionally. Shulman (1999) suggests that reflection occurs when individuals look back and consider what has occurred, reconstructing and recapturing the events that make up their daily roles – it was certainly a revealing exercise, as we discussed in Chapter 1. In recalling the cognitive (that is, what you have learnt), and also the affective (what you feel about your role), everyone undertaking reflection recaptures the events, the emotions and the achievements embedded in their daily role. Through these processes, professionals learn from their experiences and are able to consider necessary change without feelings of threat, discomfort or dismay. Reflexivity in practice is characterized by dignity and the complexity of its actions. It is worth acknowledging that reflection on professional thinking and practice is never easy. It is something that has to be worked at and often benefits from discussion with others in a similar position. Hence, we suggest peer evaluation, or linking with a 'critical colleague' as excellent processes.

To support those who feel they need an idea of a 'rating scale' or 'levels of operation', we also offer on the following pages a framework against which it is possible to evaluate oneself through four levels of overall operation. Using this construct, leaders and managers can plot themselves somewhere along a continuum (albeit subjective) so that they may, in turn, consider where they stand in relation to the contents of branches, stems and leaves. The grading system has four levels:

- Acceptable
- Good
- Very Good
- Exemplary.

These are the same categories as used in EEPES (EY) (Moyles and Musgrove 2003): it will be noted that there is no 'unacceptable' category. The reason for this is that the focus group felt strongly that anyone in a leadership and management role should be no less than 'acceptable' in that role and that most ought to achieve the 'good' level as a basic. If users cannot even mark themselves as acceptable, then it is unlikely that they will, for example, have got through a setting inspection unscathed. Some users have found the categories useful as a yardstick, but they are optional and, whilst subjective, they have been found by individual heads to be suitable for their purpose.

The four levels we have defined are intended to classify performance in a way that facilitates what is important, in other words the development of reflection and awareness.

- **Intuitive and Pragmatic**. This represents a practical stance on the role, where the head is working from a sound knowledge base, but does so intuitively, instinctively and somewhat spontaneously, rather than from the basis of deep thought or reflection.
- **Reasoned and Articulate**. This represents a more thoughtful stance, in which the head operates from the basis of thinking through and articulating the needs of any situation, using experience, sound knowledge and explanation skills.
- **Involved and Collaborative**. This represents a different level of operation altogether, where the head is much more involved in seeking expert advice from others within and beyond the setting and works in close collaboration with others whose knowledge and opinions are valued, discussed, considered and used as relevant.
- **Reflective and Philosophic**. This represents definitely the most thoughtful, cognitive level, in which one must use all one's powers of thinking to scrutinize one's beliefs and values and those of others, and explore concepts such as change and vision for one's particular setting as broadly and innovatively as possible.

These levels represent types of thinking incrementally from a basic practical stance, through to more in-depth reflective thoughts and actions. The process of reflection is a looking back at what has occurred, reconstructing, re-enacting and recapturing the events, feelings and successes. According to Hatano (1995) it is the process through which professionals learn from experience and provides the key to change in behaviours and attitudes, as well as to acquiring skills and knowledge. During the processes of reflecting, individuals will critically examine, on a regular basis, their rationales and values both about leadership and about the setting. There is no doubt that improving any setting will be a dynamic action-oriented process, likely to involve significant organizational change and offer challenge to the existing status quo. There is much evidence suggesting that engaging in reflective practice involves support, challenge and confrontation (Goodfellow 2000) – mainly the latter in relation to confronting one's own competence: never an easy task. Competence in one's role, in this case the role of head of an early years setting, is generated through high levels of professional knowledge used to analyse, evaluate and, where relevant, change the current situation. One of our heads commented: 'You don't necessarily like to identify where you're not totally competent, but you're not really satisfied with what you're doing and know that change is needed.'

Within the StEPs project (Moyles and Adams 2001) one of the benefits of reflective thinking was an enhanced sense of self-efficacy in which practitioners began to think differently about themselves. It is anticipated that, in using ELMS, although difficulties will arise for all heads in facing acknowledgement of their own strengths and weaknesses, reflection with a peer or other senior person – and the knowledge that one has great strengths in some areas – will enable the process to be undertaken with confidence as ELMS offers much support in knowing the next stages.

Reasoning and articulation of one's thinking are clearly important leadership skills if one is to persuade and encourage other staff to think in different ways about issues and challenges which confront the setting. Being involved and collaborative is also vital in early childhood care and education, particularly as many leaders double as practitioners and also have a clear role in relating to the wider community in which the setting is located.

We would suggest that users may want overall to consider their leadership and management role against these levels and reflect on where they currently 'are' and where they would like to be in a few months' time. The timescale will be dependent upon individuals and what they are trying to achieve in their settings.

At its heart, ELMS offers detailed information about what an early years head needs to address in fulfilling the daily role to a high standard. It cannot give evidence about every angle because settings and leaders differ. But it is as comprehensive as we could make it and offers its users a useful overall framework for determining their existing and potential leadership and management traits. Different people will succeed in different ways within different components: that is the nature of the job, as we have seen via the literature review in the Introduction. Some will excel in some branches, stems and leaves; others will find challenges that need to be addressed. The 'secret', if there is one, is to be honest and realistic with oneself about one's own capabilities. You are only fooling yourself if you under- or overestimate them.

Undertaking the evaluation

Evaluation is undertaken through close scrutiny of the leaves. This is done by working through a series of reflective questions:

1. What are your strengths?
2. What is your evidence for this identification of strengths?
3. Which areas do you feel currently need improvement?
4. Why are these important to you and the setting?
5. What can you do to build on your strengths/advance your professional competence?
6. What do you need to do to extend and enhance your skills and capabilities?
7. What is necessary to ensure that the qualities, characteristics and traits you possess are used appropriately for the setting?
8. Are you being realistic?

(A shortened version of this is included in each of the individual stems and branches but users can return to these more extended questions to prompt additional thinking.)

In examining the leaves in this way, users will also be able to determine the level at which they are currently operating and decide whether particular areas need to be reconsidered. We would advise users not simply to deem everything the first time round as 'acceptable' (as many users seemed to want to do). All heads know they have particular strengths and these should be identified and celebrated. Our focus group felt that there were several phases to the self-evaluation:

1. Read through the whole document to familiarize yourself with the various branches, stems and leaves.
2. Read through again, identifying particular areas where you have strengths (those which appear to be very good and exemplary): this promotes a sense of well-being and adds encouragement for the next stage.

In each of these stages, you need to think carefully what evidence you would offer to another (peer-) evaluator (or just to yourself) to be able to show that these indeed are your strengths.

3. Read through again and identify which stem needs the greatest amount of thought or action, that is, the one in which you shine the least.
4. Isolate aspects of this stem in which you are acceptable or good.
5. Decide how you will improve your skills, attitudes and understanding of these areas. It may be necessary to think first about whether there are particular

constraints (of knowledge, practice, culture or policy) which make this stem particularly challenging.

It is as well to work on only one stem at a time, otherwise the task can be overwhelming. Users can give themselves a timescale in which to gradually work through all the stems – perhaps even a whole year, but this will depend on the time set aside to devote to the self-evaluation and other factors such as whether you are undertaking NPQICL or other training. Remember first to congratulate yourself on those stems and leaves in which you show strengths: don't dwell on those which present challenges – be proactive and make yourself a plan for improvement rather than getting out the big stick.

This process helps to acknowledge in an honest and open way those things which do need improvement. The levels and their explanations are as follows:

- **Level 1: ACCEPTABLE – Intuitive and Pragmatic**. This level of operation is undertaken with a basic level of cognition and reflection. If questioned about their work, heads operating at this level answer in descriptive rather than analytical terms; they rarely question the appropriateness of their particular approach and defend it with statements such as 'That's just the way it is' and 'It's the way I've always done it.' At this level, there is some recognition of choice (of being aware of other ways of doing things) and purpose (believing that the way they do things is the most effective way). This level can be summarized by the statement 'I do . . .', in other words it is a managerial approach that is individual rather than interpersonal, with minimum discernible reflection and reasoning.

- **Level 2: GOOD – Reasoned and Articulate**. This level of operation is undertaken with a medium level of cognition and reflection but with a limited willingness to involve others and be collaborative. If questioned about their work, heads operating at this level answer in analytical, not just descriptive, terms; they also question the appropriateness of their particular approach and rationalize it in some way. At this level, there is some recognition of choice (of being aware of other ways of doing things) and purpose (believing that the way they do things is the most effective way). This level can be summarized by the statement 'I do because . . .', in other words it is an approach to management that is individual rather than interpersonal, with a moderate level of reflection and informed reasoning.

- **Level 3: VERY GOOD – Involved and Collaborative**. This level of operation is undertaken with fairly extensive cognition and reflection and with a determination to involve others in leadership as a collaborative venture. If interviewed about their work, leaders and managers operating at this level answer in analytical terms; they also question the appropriateness of their particular approach and are able to defend it, rather than rationalize it, in some way. At this level, there is some informed recognition of choice (of being aware of other ways of doing things) and purpose (believing that the way they do things is the most effective way), and some consideration of the ethical implications of practice. This level can be summarized by the statement 'We do . . .', in other words it is an approach to leadership and management that is interpersonal rather than individual, with a good level of critical reflection and informed reasoning.

- **Level 4: EXEMPLARY – Reflective and Philosophic**. This level of operation is undertaken with extensive cognition and reflection, and a strong willingness to involve others, collaborate and reflect continually on leadership and management competences. Evidence of the head's excellence is manifest everywhere in the setting. If interviewed about their leadership and management approaches, those operating at this level answer in reflective and analytical terms; they also interrogate the appropriateness of their particular approach and inevitably rationalize it in some way. At the exemplary level there is a sophisticated understanding of both choice (of being aware of other ways of doing things) and purpose (believing that the way they do things is the most effective way). As well as this, a consideration of the global, ethical, cultural and political implications of their practice is evident. This level can be summarized by the statement 'We do because …', in other words it is an approach to leadership that is interpersonal, with an exceptional level of reflection, reasoning, cognition and conceptualization.

These four levels offer a graded approach to exploring individual head's current strengths and support the recognition of needs. For example, a head may be at the exemplary level in the leaves related to 'being responsible for, and thoughtful about, basic needs' (1.2), but only be acceptable in 'being visionary' (1.1), thus offering direction in terms of necessary improvements. More is written about the meaning of individual items in the text which accompanies each branch, stem and leaf.

If the head chooses to use the grading system, it is up to that individual to plot the appropriate level of operation along the continuum without being either self-effacing or overconfident. ELMS is perhaps best used in the presence of other staff, drawing on their feedback and utilizing their presence to 'referee' the evaluation.

'Tree surgery'

We call this section 'tree surgery' because really it is about deciding, having completed your evaluation, what 'treatment' is needed in particular sections to extend and enhance the levels of operation within the branches, stems and leaves. This may involve the user in:

- identifying specific training needs;
- talking through the challenges with a mentor (if one is available);
- identifying some books or articles that will offer support in this area;
- talking with particular members of staff;
- consulting with settings managers or an LEA adviser;
- identifying particular training needs; …

These are just a few of the myriad ways in which one can find support for dealing with identified needs.

As we have seen, evaluating practice using the ELMS tree has many functions. For example, through this process, troubleshooting – working out where your problems and challenges lie and which professional areas need developing – is relatively simple and enjoyable. It is also easy to go on a 'guilt trip' and assume that one should be good at everything. This is both demoralizing and unrealistic. As Fink (2005: xx) suggests, the lists or templates that exist 'seem to require people of heroic abilities to lead [settings]. … [S]uch lists promote guilt … martyrdom … or the compliant messenger.' Our intention is none of these. Rather we want to produce

> successful leaders [who] do not learn to 'do' leadership and then stick to set patterns and ways of doing things along a prescribed set of known rules. They are willing to change in response to new sets of circumstances – and to the differing needs of children … and teachers.
>
> (Riley and MacBeath (2003: 174)

Johnson (1999: 9) emphasizes the need for an evidence base, pointing out that in order to meet leadership challenges effectively, heads

> must be clear about their own personal contribution to the achievement of schools' goals and targets. Setting goals for success at an individual level can be an effective way of ensuring the necessary levels of motivation and commitment to guarantee success. Personal goal setting helps [heads] clarify priorities.

As part of self- or peer evaluation purposes, it is also necessary, then, to list your targets and formulate an action plan. In relation to the above, this means asking:

- What TARGETS need setting in order to make the head more 'responsible for basic needs'?
- What ACTION will be needed in order to achieve a higher level next?

Johnson (1999: 16) asks: 'What evidence will you be able to see, hear and feel which will let you know you have achieved [your targets] ... what on-going feedback will let you know you are making progress towards your goals?' The layout of ELMS is such that these aspects are incorporated into the evaluation sheets which accompany the branches in each of the next four chapters.

The questions on the right-hand page of the ELMS tree layout ask for in-depth consideration of the contents of each leaf. More space is likely to be needed to explore the questions they pose, so the manager in question can use an evaluation notebook when completing these sections.

The cameos

For some of the more challenging stems on the ELMS tree, additional information is provided in the form of cameos produced in close association with our research group. These cameos seek to contextualize the leaves that make up each stem and bring to life and elaborate each quality, skill, attribute, characteristic and associated attitudes inherent within specific stems. In their way, the cameos represent diaries or accounts of individual heads and their daily lives. Keeping such daily diaries (if perhaps more brief) could support heads in gaining a sense of achievement as they work towards higher levels of the ELMS tree. We all know how easy it is to get caught up in the minutiae of each day and not feel any sense of accomplishment or satisfaction at the end: just a sense that one must do more tomorrow! Our time is finite and has to be used to best effect. Each issue such as this will be explored within the appropriate branch.

What, then, are the components of the ELMS tree?

To give a clear outline of the components, we have listed them in the following pages as an Index, prior to presenting the branches, stems and leaves in each of the next four chapters with their accompanying cameos and explanations. In each case the main headings are the branches – the stems – represented by the initial decimalized numbers (1.1, 1.2, 1.3 etc.), and the leaves have both the decimal number of the stem and an individual letter (2.1a, 2.1b, 2.1c etc.). It is worth reiterating that the division of ELMS into four sections is an attempt to make it more useable and logical as an evaluation scheme. Some overlap is therefore unavoidable but considered useful by the research group.

The ELMS tree typology

Leadership Qualities branch

1.1   Be visionary
    1.1a   Offer direction and guidance
    1.1b   Offer destinations, structure and compromise

1.2   Be responsible for, and thoughtful about, basic needs
    1.2a   Be responsible for the safety and well-being of the children
    1.2b   Be responsible for the safety and well-being of the staff
    1.2c   Be responsible for the basic needs of the setting and create a culture and climate conducive to learning for everyone

1.3   Be accountable
    1.3a   Provide quality childcare and education services and ensure that quality assurance measures are in place
    1.3b   Understand and apply appropriate disciplinary procedures for children
    1.3c   Understand and apply appropriate disciplinary procedures for staff
    1.3d   Be able to handle complaints and other procedures that require understanding, diplomacy and tact
    1.3e   Be accountable TO and FOR own actions and those of others

1.4   Be a leader
    1.4a   Be charismatic
    1.4b   Have integrity and justified confidence
    1.4c   Be able to engage and involve others in ideas, innovations, goals and visions, and to compromise where relevant
    1.4d   Command respect and offer respect
    1.4e   Be able to motivate and persuade staff
    1.4f   Persevere with understanding and developing the leadership role

1.5   Be flexible and versatile
    1.5a   View early years leadership as interchangeable, a situational phenomenon
    1.5b   View change as a positive occurrence and respond confidently
    1.5c   Take risks based on clear understanding of the situation

1.6   Be knowledgeable and be an informational resource for the staff
    1.6a   Have knowledge and understanding of child development and child psychology
    1.6b   Have knowledge and understanding of different curricula, both broad and specific national requirements
    1.6c   Have knowledge and understanding of related local policy and initiatives
    1.6d   Have knowledge and understanding of current legislation and national policy initiatives

1.7   Understand the importance of shared values
    1.7a   Be able to generate shared values amongst staff within the setting
    1.7b   Ensure that neither staff nor children develop negative or harmful values or traits, such as prejudice and stereotyping
    1.7c   Ensure that the culture, the direction and the destination of the setting are built into its organizational framework
    1.7d   Ensure that all members of staff and all parents feel included and valued

1.8   Understand how to lead and manage change
- 1.8a   Have a positive attitude to change and compromise
- 1.8b   Be proactive rather than reactive to change
- 1.8c   Have the wisdom to identify the need for change from within and anticipate the demand for change from outside
- 1.8d   Implement relevant changes sensitively whilst involving and reassuring staff and parents
- 1.8e   Know how to support staff, parents and children following change
- 1.8f   Be aware of the effect that change, coming from the home or the setting, can have on children

1.9   Ensure that all relevant people are empowered and enabled
- 1.9a   Empower and enable children
- 1.9b   Empower and enable staff
- 1.9c   Empower and enable parents and understand the multiple roles and responsibilities they have towards their child(ren)

1.10   Earn status and rank as a culture setter
- 1.10a   Know how to create an ethos appropriate for the setting
- 1.10b   Understand the culture of organizations specifically and universally
- 1.10c   Cultivate and represent the defining essence of the setting
- 1.10d   Ensure that values and ethics are identified and defined within the setting

Management Skills branch

2.1   Ensure effective human resource management and administration
- 2.1a   Be a competent organizer and know how to assign staff, ensuring that they are well matched to their tasks
- 2.1b   Be an effective recruiter and retainer of staff, ensuring that staff numbers are optimum
- 2.1c   Be an effective appraiser of staff, being encouraging, supportive, firm and constructively critical where necessary
- 2.1d   Be an effective motivator and supporter of staff, giving them energy and instilling their work with meaning and value
- 2.1e   Ensure that staff have appropriate professional development opportunities
- 2.1f   Ensure good working relations and networking with staff and amongst staff
- 2.1g   Ensure good relations with parents and the community and encourage staff to do the same
- 2.1h   Ensure appropriate authority is maintained whilst offering democratic approaches to others
- 2.1i   Ensure staff feel included and responsible, optimizing their performance and well-being
- 2.1j   Ensure good practice is recognized and poor practice is moderated

2.2   Ensure effective curriculum management
- 2.2a   Ensure effective and appropriate curriculum planning
- 2.2b   Ensure effective and appropriate curriculum implementation
- 2.2c   Ensure effective and appropriate curriculum evaluation
- 2.2d   Manage and lead effective and appropriate curriculum change
- 2.2e   Promote consistent and appropriate daily curriculum routines for staff and children

2.3   Ensure effective interaction, involvement and intervention at setting level
    2.3a   Understand the relationship between parents and staff as one of partnership and mutual benefit
    2.3b   Fulfil the responsibility of supporting the education of parents as well as children
    2.3c   Undertake good two-way communication to ensure parity of approach and philosophy between staff and parents
    2.3d   Recognize and utilize the different but complementary expertise of differentially trained staff and of parents
    2.3e   Appreciate that parents have a key role in determining the level of professional recognition received by the setting and the early years profession

2.4   Ensure effective interaction, involvement and intervention at local level
    2.4a   Understand the relationship of the child to the local community and, for example, its range of ethnic groups and languages
    2.4b   Stay abreast of local policy and related issues that may have an impact upon the setting and/or the profession
    2.4c   Know how the political scene operates and who is involved at local level
    2.4d   Raise the profile of the setting and/or the profession within the local community
    2.4e   Store and catalogue all relevant local/regional documents in a suitable location so as to be accessible for others
    2.4f   Market the setting and/or the profession effectively to the local community

2.5   Ensure effective interaction, involvement and intervention at national and international level
    2.5a   Understand the relationship of the child to the national/international community
    2.5b   Stay abreast of government policy, research and related issues that may have an impact upon the setting and/or the profession
    2.5c   Know how the political scene operates and who is involved at national level
    2.5d   Endeavour to raise the profile of the setting and/or the profession within the national/international community
    2.5e   Keep abreast of national/international research which can inform practice and thinking

2.6   Ensure effective decision making
    2.6a   Ensure appropriate delegation of responsibilities for making decisions
    2.6b   Delegate with responsibility; ensure that the people to whom a task is delegated understands its parameters and their responsibilities
    2.6c   Make decisions explicit and inclusive where possible so that others have confidence in them
    2.6d   Make decisions based on the vision of the setting, its direction and its destination

2.7   Ensure effective planning and strategy making
    2.7a   Be adept at short-term planning to support the smooth running of the setting on a daily basis

2.7b   Be adept at long-term planning to ensure the fulfilment of the vision of the future of the setting

2.7c   Understand the value of curriculum planning and be adept at undertaking this for the benefit of both children and staff

2.7d   Ensure that the curriculum provides continuity between the home and the setting and between the setting and school

2.8   Ensure effective implementation and monitoring of ideas

2.8a   Ensure that plans are implemented efficiently and effectively

2.8b   Ensure that deviations from plans are well conceived and decisions are made explicit

2.8c   Monitor all actions to ensure that the planning and implementation of ideas is analysed and evaluated

2.8d   Understand inspection requirements and compliance issues

2.9   Ensure effective operation of basic administrative procedures

2.9a   Understand procedures for the admission and registration of children

2.9b   Understand the need for, and the implementation of, appropriate records of children and staff

2.9c   Understand how to budget effectively and appreciate the importance of securing funding, financial planning and transparent accounting

2.10   Ensure effective physical resource management and administration

2.10a   Ensure acquisition and effective utilization of resources

2.10b   Have knowledge of strategies for systematic resourcing and implement them

2.10c   Ensure effective financial management

2.10d   Use the budget appropriately to provide optimally for children, staff and parents

2.10e   Take responsibility for the physical environment

2.10f   Have a special interest in the learning and teaching environment and ensure consensus amongst all involved

2.10g   Ensure a safe and healthy learning and working environment

Professional Skills and Attributes branch

3.1   Promote the formalization of staff qualifications

3.1a   Have a high level of formal accreditation relevant to early years management

3.1b   Promote and support staff to achieve a high level of accreditation relevant to the early years profession

3.1c   Ensure that self and staff have the opportunity for ongoing and relevant professional development

3.1d   Ensure that adequate resources, time and money are invested in staff and their training

3.2   Be an effective problem solver

3.2a   Be able to recognize, identify and diagnose problems

3.2b   Be able to solve problems and facilitate problem solving amongst others

3.2c   Be reflective about own leadership and managerial role to ensure that the process of self-improvement is continuous and enhances performance

3.3   Have efficient time management skills

3.3a   Have the ability to prioritize actions for self and others

3.3b   Ensure time is used effectively and disruptions kept to a minimum

3.3c   Promote punctuality and ensure staff meet deadlines

3.3d   Ensure effective handling and dissemination of paperwork

3.4   Have good communication and discourse skills

3.4a   Promote high quality and effective communication between management and staff

3.4b   Promote high quality and effective communication between staff and children

3.4c   Have excellent oral and written communication skills

3.4d   Promote friendly and sensitive communication and networking

3.4e   Promote accurate understanding through discussion and explanation

3.4f   Be an active listener and a sensitive, empathic responder

3.4g   Promote honest but sensitive communication between staff and management

3.4h   Promote responsive, sensitive and friendly communication with parents

3.4i   Ensure mutually beneficial communication with the wider community

3.4j   Ensure that children, staff, parents and the wider community are all well-informed and involved

3.5   Have excellent diplomacy and conflict resolution skills

3.5a   Be receptive to suggestions

3.5b   Negotiate, respect and utilize different viewpoints

3.5c   Listen actively to staff and undertake necessary mediation

3.5d   Listen actively to parents and undertake necessary mediation

3.5e   Listen actively to children

3.5f   Resolve tensions between individuals and understand compromise

3.5g   Be capable of identifying, resolving and, where relevant, averting conflict

3.5h   Understand internal conflicts and how they can be negotiated/resolved

3.5i   Take a calm, positive and tolerant approach to conflicts and crises

Personal Characteristics and Attitudes branch

4.1   Have knowledge of, and a natural enthusiasm for children, teaching and learning

4.1a   Understand and value the dual responsibility of early years providers to care, to ensure learning and to teach

4.1b   Understand the concept of 'in loco parentis'

4.1c   Understand children as intelligent but vulnerable

4.1d   Understand children as independent and individual

4.1e   Conceptualize each child as a unique individual

4.1f   Conceptualize children as family members

4.1g   Conceptualize children as community members

4.2   Have a strong commitment to the settings-to-school transitions of the child

4.2a   Ensure the essential social progress of the child

4.2b   Ensure the essential academic progress of the child

4.2c   Have strong background experience and understanding of children

4.2d   Cultivate good relations and communications with the schools to which the children will transfer

4.3   Have an attraction to the profession for intrinsic rather than extrinsic reasons

4.3a   Be interested in, and fulfil the important components of, the job as specific to early years

4.3b   Fulfil with interest and commitment the important components of the job in relation to leadership, management and administration

4.3c   Understand the universal components of the role of head of setting

4.4   Have a continued commitment to, and vested interest in, children's overall development

4.4a   Understand the intellectual/cognitive development of children

4.4b   Understand the physical development of children, including both fine-motor and gross-motor skills

4.4c   Understand the social and cultural development of children

4.4d   Understand the emotional and spiritual development of children

4.5   Have a strong sense of ambition and a strong desire for improvement

4.5a   Have a commitment to long-term self-improvement

4.5b   Have a desire to improve the social/communicative self

4.5c   Have a desire to improve the professional self

4.5d   Have a desire to improve the setting and have realistic and appropriate ambitions for it

4.5e   Have an infectious and dynamic sense of ambition

4.5f   Relay and instil ambition in the staff

4.5g   Relay and instil ambition in the children

4.6   Have an approach that advocates creative intelligence

4.6a   Promote the holistic development and expression of the creative capacity of children

4.6b   Promote the holistic development and expression of the creative capacity of staff

4.6c   Promote innovative and individual approaches by staff

4.6d   Understand children as builders and constructors

4.6e   Understand children as alternative communicators

4.7   Have an approach that advocates emotional intelligence

4.7a   Be able to adopt a task-leader style when necessary

4.7b   Be able to adopt a relationship-leader style when necessary

4.7c   Be aware of the potential of employing and utilizing, rather than stifling, emotions

4.7d   Have an emotional but stable personal approach to personnel

4.7e   Understand the reasons for stress and learn to turn stress to one's advantage

4.8   Have an infectious (self-)awareness

4.8a   Be aware of environmental issues and practise eco-friendly procedures and policies

4.8b   Be aware of sex, gender, race, faith and ethical issues

4.8c   Be aware of staff and employment issues, including equal opportunities and other equality issues

4.8d   Have sensitive regard for children, their ethnic backgrounds and their self-concepts

4.8e   Have sensitive regard for staff, their ethnic backgrounds and their self-concepts

4.8f   Have an empathic awareness of the overall needs of children

4.8g   Have an empathic awareness of the overall needs of staff

4.8h   Be aware of, and embrace, new technologies and new media

4.8i   Be aware of equal opportunities and discrimination issues related to sex, age, race and ethnicity

4.8j   Be aware of equal opportunities and discrimination issues related to staff, children and parents with special needs

4.9   Have a good sense of humour and understand the importance of play and having fun

4.9a   Promote effective and appropriate use of humour in the setting

4.9b   Maximize humour as an aid to learning and teaching

4.9c   Understand the relationship humour has with motivation, attention and concentration

4.9d   Understand the relationship play has with motivation, attention and concentration and promote learning through a play-based curriculum

4.9e   Understand the role of play in cultivating the investigative and first-hand experiences of children

4.9f   Cultivate an environment where children learn moderation and restraint

4.9g   Understand play as an important social and cognitive activity in which some children (and adults) require support to engage and interact

3 The Leadership Qualities branch

Introduction

Leadership is an important theme in the early years and is currently the subject of much scholarly debate and activity internationally. For early years heads, having the qualities of a competent and effective leader is important for the well-being of children, staff and parents with whom heads come into contact. But defining it, as we have seen, is problematical, particularly given the unprecedented changes that are happening continuously (Fullan 2001), especially in the early years field.

To add to the challenges, there has seemingly been reluctance on the part of early years heads to conceptualize themselves as leaders – as Caldwell (2003) suggests, many are loathe to see themselves in this role – despite now running business enterprises, which is what modern early years settings have become (Smith and Langston 1999). Moreover, early years heads often operate without the support of either training or continuous professional development to which heads in schools and other businesses have ready access, which could mean that they are 'significantly under-prepared for their role' (Muijs *et al.* 2004: 160). It has only been with the advent of the NPQICL in England that such training has been available, and then not necessarily widespread at present. The unwillingness of early years heads to embrace a full leadership role may, in part, be due to the connotations of 'management' and its associations with power, authority and hierarchy; not conducive in a climate where everyone 'mucks in together' and is considered equal. A reluctance to accept and celebrate differential roles has been prominent in early childhood for many years (see, for example, Moyles and Suschitzky 1996).

Early years leadership is somewhat unique in that it is concerned mainly with the leadership of women – and mainly women leading women-dominated teams. As we have seen, however, in the preceding chapters, how we conceptualize leaders and leadership continues to change rapidly and the concept of feminine and masculine traits has been somewhat overruled in favour of leadership as a 'function within the organisational setting which can be performed by a particular individual ... or by individuals appropriate to particular situations or issues' (Bennett *et al.* 2003: x). This collegial approach to leadership is generally favoured by early years heads but, in some ways, makes the concept of effective leader even more characterized by elusive qualities that are difficult to define and quantify: the first of these is *charisma* (1.4a) (see Fatt 2000 and Paul *et al.* 2002 for further discussion).

Two qualities on which there is a consensus are *vision* (1.1) and *respect* (1.4d). Smith and Langston (1999: 14) explain that 'Having vision means being able to articulate your own philosophy to a range of people'. We would add, having the confidence to do so and respecting other people's views. Vision also needs perseverance (1.4e) – it is unlikely that everyone in a setting will immediately share the same ideals and the head will need to persevere in enabling everyone to come to a clear understanding of the setting's current and future thinking and direction. Vision is something that should be articulated clearly – it may emanate from the head or be a shared venture (the latter is preferable according to much leadership literature). Vision requires a set of *shared values* (1.7) and a shared philosophy amongst staff: in the best settings they share common ground and common understandings. Sometimes, without it ever being made explicit, all members of staff know exactly what their setting is 'about' and where it is going: this frequently happens when staff have worked together for a long time. It is quite an interesting activity to articulate what this shared vision means – sometimes there is not as much unity as appears on the surface.

As well as being inspirational and charismatic, leadership is also about being *responsible* (1.2) and *accountable* (1.3). Such qualities can be learnt, but they are often intrinsic and reflect the kind of person who is comfortable with an early years leadership role. An effective early years head has a keen sense of responsibility and accountability, with feet firmly on the ground; she does not lead staff off on flights of fancy: she is good at communicating and also good at putting plans into action. Needless to say, *flexibility* and *versatility* (1.5), especially having the ability to adopt and adapt to different approaches, is of paramount importance. Leaders need also to be risk takers, pushing themselves and everyone that bit further from the basis of clear knowledge and understanding of early childhood care and education as it relates to that particular setting (1.5c).

The other indispensable quality required for good leadership is *knowledge* and being able to function as an *informational resource* for staff (1.6). Leaders should maximize their knowledge of all aspects of the profession, such as child development and child psychology, various curricula, regional and national education policies, and relevant legislation. At least, a willingness and ability to learn is a must.

Leadership is something that should not fall solely on the head. Believing it should may explain some of the reluctance on the part of early years heads to fully identify with the term 'leader' as it threatens to take away the leadership and accountability of other members of staff. As Smith and Langston (1999: 19) suggest, 'leadership is never just one way'. Therefore, engendering *shared values* (1.7) and the being able to lead and manage *change* (1.8) with the full co-operation of staff are crucial leadership skills. A major corollary of professionalism is change: in education and care, change is one of the few certainties. In such a climate a competent and effective early years head must understand how to lead change. As Jackson says (2003: xvii), 'The role of the "leader" ... is to harness, focus, liberate, empower and align ... leadership towards common purposes.' Change needs to be seen as a challenge not a threat by everyone: it requires:

- communication and sharing of information;
- commitment from all staff;
- control opportunities for all staff;
- leaders to build staff confidence in the outcomes;
- expert advice from others – it is a strength not a weakness to ask for help.

Seen like this, change can become *empowering*, allowing colleagues, children and parents to make their own marks upon the setting (1.9) and to feel comfortable about commenting on values and necessary changes. This includes taking an enabling approach, whereby obstacles are minimized and everyone adopts a 'can do' approach. Indeed, in such a demanding and varied working environment, having staff who are united and who feel that enhancement of their roles is an expectation is also vital.

Just as importantly, perhaps, it is the wise leader who recognizes that s/he is a *culture setter* (1.10) but that this needs an empathic approach to others who have their own values and cultures, particularly the children for whom the culture of the school can be quite alien (see Brooker 2002). The culture of any setting can be reflected in something as simple as the types and content of displays. Do they, for example, reflect the ethnic background of the children and staff or encourage thinking about other cultures? Are they changed frequently to reflect current interests of staff and children? Do they promote (and even question) what is happening in the local and national cultural frameworks?

In the midst of all this, heads should recognize that they are human (see Fink's comments in the Introduction). An effective early years head cannot know everything, is not always right, and is not always in control: but they are willing to learn and moderate their leadership ideas and actions. Expecting perfection from oneself as a head will almost certainly lead to feelings of inadequacy: believing one is, or should be, flawless may not have a positive effect on the setting and the quality of the childcare service. Perhaps being realistic should be added to the typology!

Dispersed throughout the rest of this chapter are the detailed stems and leaves, exemplified where relevant by cameos and additional theoretical support. The first cameo relates to vision.

Stem 1.1 Be visionary

Cameo: Leanne

Leanne is the manager of a large state nursery. When asked what she considers to be the most important attribute required for effective early years leadership, she answers, 'being able to communicate and to involve people in a vision of what the nursery is currently like and what we want it to be.'

Indeed, vision is incredibly important. 'Without vision, our nursery would have no ambition, or it would have competing ambitions, which is nearly as bad. There would be no shared philosophy between staff, and decision making would be a nightmare.'

Knowingly or not, Leanne has touched on two different types of vision. Firstly, there is vision in the sense of a mission or position statement, a declaration of the values, beliefs and aims of the setting. 'The problem with a mission statement is that what you value and believe in as a professional changes almost on a daily basis. There is so much research going on, so many social, political and economic changes happening, that you can't afford to have static values and beliefs. You can have a basic aim, such as "to provide quality childcare," or something like that. What you really need, though, is to have a shared philosophy, a point of reference so that heads can make informed decisions that represent the interests of everyone involved.' The values, beliefs and aims of early years providers change in accordance with such things as the local area, the number of the staff and the extent of the budget. These need to be made explicit.

This type of vision may be the brainchild of the head. This is fine, so long as the vision is not at odds with that of the rest of the staff. 'The head may play the role of main developer and "keeper" of the vision, but the key thing is that everyone is involved and represented, parents as well as staff.' This type of visionary leadership can be classified by the term 'direction,' that is, providing the nursery with a clear and purposeful direction, an attitude rather than an actual physical vision of the future. An effective early years leader, therefore, should offer direction (1.1a) for the setting. The other type of vision refers to an actual achievable conception or forecast of the future – clear targets and goals, that is, for a dynamic future. This kind of vision may include plans for expansion, diversification, extension of staff, of materials or resources, and such like. This type of visionary leadership can be classified by the term 'destination' (knowing where one is going). An effective early years head, therefore, should also offer destinations (1.1b) for the setting.

As one example, Figure 3.1 is the position statement of an early years institution, stating explicitly its direction and intended destination (Robson and Smedley 1996: vii).

EARLY CHILDHOOD CENTRE

ROEHAMPTON INSTITUTE LONDON

POSITION STATEMENT

The purpose of the centre is to promote and foster early childhood philosophy, practice and profile, through enquiry and dialogue based upon the following principles:

- The child is a 'going concern'
- The child is a 'meaning maker'
- The child's understandings arise from and are embedded in a social context
- A distinction is made between education for understanding which is transferable; and education as the acquisition of inert bodies of knowledge
- The way that we teach children influences their present attitudes to learning and their future learning
- Equality of opportunity is not just an interesting option: it is an imperative
- Teaching is most effective when it is based upon observation of children and recognises that:
  - parents and other professionals concerned with the care and education of young children have important insights and contributions to make to learning and development
  - education and care interpenetrate in early childhood needs

Figure 3.1   Example of a position statement. From Robson and Smedley (1996: vii)

Stem 1.1	Leaves 1.1a–1.1b

An effective early years leader or manager should . . .

1.1 Be visionary	*1.1a Offer direction and guidance (this involves making the values, beliefs and aims of the setting explicit and accessible so that there is a clear stance and philosophy that can be used as a basis for making, guiding and supporting decisions)*

	1.1b Offer destinations, structure and compromise (this involves setting achievable physical targets and goals for improvement and having an explicit and well-conceived vision of the future – unlike direction, it is actual rather than attitudinal)

List your targets	
Formulate an action plan	

Reflect on your capabilities and complete the boxes...

What are your strengths?
Which areas need improvement?
What can you do to build on your strengths?
What do you need to do to improve your skills and
capabilities?

What are your strengths?
Which areas need improvement?
What can you do to build on your strengths?
What do you need to do to improve your skills and
capabilities?

Use this space for writing

Use this space for writing

Use this space for writing

Stem 1.2 Be responsible

The hierarchy of needs

In essence, being responsible for the safety, health and well-being of staff, children and others within the early years setting is about understanding what they all need individually and collectively and then providing it. So what do they need? Maslow (1943) suggested the hierarchy shown in Figure 3.2 (read from bottom to top). The relevance of this diagram to early years heads is outlined further below.

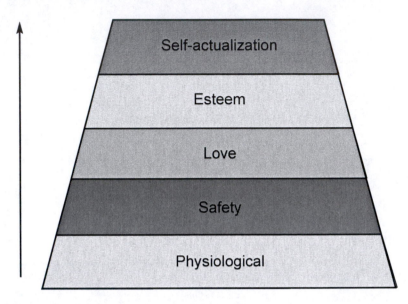

Figure 3.2   Maslow's hierarchy of needs

An effective early years leader should have a working knowledge of what motivates children and staff, and what they need. Indeed, Maslow proposed that people are motivated by their needs, which are specific to each individual. He claimed that people need their physiological needs satisfied first, such as food and shelter (stage one), then they need their safety needs satisfied, such as freedom from danger (stage two). They then need their emotional needs satisfied, such as social acceptance (stage three), followed by their esteem needs, such as having self-esteem and being esteemed by others (stage four). The last stage (stage five) is called self-actualization, which refers to achieving one's full potential and becoming content. The first four stages he called 'deficiency needs,' so stage five is where every need is satisfied and there is no longer any deficiency, hence contentment.

Having in-depth knowledge of Maslow's theory may not appear immediately important to effective early years leadership. However, it is essential to have some understanding of human motivation. For example, why does a child cry? Is s/he hungry, thirsty, hot or cold? No. Does s/he feel threatened or in danger? No. Does s/he feel excluded from the activity? Yes, it appears to be so. The child is at the third stage. This ability to determine first why someone in the setting is responding as they are and secondly to know what can be provided to help is crucial, with staff as well as children.

There is a member of staff, say, who is not acting her usual self. She is not hungry or thirsty. She is comfortable. She is not in any danger. She works amongst some of her best friends at the setting. Perhaps, then, she is not feeling as though she is doing her job quite as well as she could. Perhaps she has low self-esteem or feels she is not highly esteemed within the structure. Perhaps this is because she is not receiving enough support, praise or encouragement from the leader?

Of course, not every incident can be dealt with so easily. Problems cannot be solved through such a crude process of deduction. Human nature is not that simple to understand. However, what is important is an awareness of the common ground we all share as human beings – our basic needs. We are all, in Maslow's words, 'needs junkies'. An effective early years head, therefore, should have at least some knowledge of behavioural theories to help them ensure that children and staff feel fulfilled and important in the setting by having their needs met.

Stem 1.2	**Leaves 1.2a–1.2c**

An effective early years leader or manager should...

1.2 Be responsible for, and thoughtful about, basic needs	*1.2a Be responsible for the safety and well-being of the children (this involves ensuring that all staff share the same sense of responsibility and that the learning environment is both safe and stimulating)*

	1.2b Be responsible for the safety and well-being of the staff (this involves ensuring that the teaching environment is both safe and stimulating for staff, who have feelings of ownership and empowerment)

	1.2c Be responsible for the basic needs of the setting and create a culture and climate conducive to learning for everyone (this involves both human and material subjects, such as budget, bids for funding, record-keeping, and policy development, such as admissions and accidents)

List your targets	
Formulate an action plan	

Reflect on your capabilities and complete the boxes...

What are your strengths?
Which areas need improvement?
What can you do to build on your strengths?
What do you need to do to improve your skills and
capabilities?

What are your strengths?
Which areas need improvement?
What can you do to build on your strengths?
What do you need to do to improve your skills and
capabilities?

What are your strengths?
Which areas need improvement?
What can you do to build on your strengths?
What do you need to do to improve your skills and
capabilities?

Use this space for writing

Use this space for writing

Stem 1.3	Leaves 1.3a–1.3e

An effective early years leader or manager should...

1.3 Be accountable	*1.3a Provide quality childcare and education services and ensure that quality assurance measures are in place (this involves having ambition, goals and strategies for continual improvement, as well as taking formal quality assurance measures)*

	1.3b Understand and apply appropriate disciplinary procedures for children (this involves knowing about child psychology and the legal position of early years professionals, and having clear procedures to follow)

	1.3c Understand and apply appropriate disciplinary procedures for staff (this involves making codes of behaviour and standards for performance explicit, as well as having the necessary support programmes)

	1.3d Be able to handle complaints and other procedures that require understanding, diplomacy and tact (this involves having excellent interpersonal skills and having the ability to calm heated interactions)

	1.3e Be accountable TO and FOR own actions and those of others (this involves being accountable TO management committees, governing bodies and parents, etc., and accountable FOR material subjects, such as transparent systems)

List your targets	
Formulate an action plan	

Reflect on your capabilities and complete the boxes ...

What are your strengths?
Which areas need improvement?
What can you do to build on your strengths?
What do you need to do to improve your skills and
capabilities?

What are your strengths?
Which areas need improvement?
What can you do to build on your strengths?
What do you need to do to improve your skills and
capabilities?

What are your strengths?
Which areas need improvement?
What can you do to build on your strengths?
What do you need to do to improve your skills and
capabilities?

What are your strengths?
Which areas need improvement?
What can you do to build on your strengths?
What do you need to do to improve your skills and
capabilities?

What are your strengths?
Which areas need improvement?
What can you do to build on your strengths?
What do you need to do to improve your skills and
capabilities?

Stem 1.4 Be a leader

Cameo: Elaine

'I'm not talking about having the same qualities as celebrities and television personalities, but having the right kind of charisma is really important. I've worked for heads who have no charisma at all. You just don't feel the same desire to achieve, and the atmosphere is not as it should or could be. Of course, I've also worked for heads who are brilliant and have loads of charisma. You have intense feelings towards them, they galvanize you into action; they always have energy, time and ideas. How would I personally define charisma? I'm not sure. It is really difficult to pin down. I'd say it's about being naturally likeable and energetic, but also being able to make people listen to you, not because you force them to but because they want to.'

There are many qualities needed to be an effective leader, charisma being one of the most important. Indeed, much has been written in recent years on 'charismatic leadership' (see, for example, Paul *et al.* 2002). Theorists tend to characterize charisma as comprising three constituent parts: being a gifted leader, having the natural ability to command loyalty and respect from people, and popularity. Leaders described as charismatic, transformational or visionary appear to generate highly committed followers and to make personal sacrifices above and beyond the call of duty. Such leaders seem to have very positive effects upon their organizations and to generate internal moral standards within the organization.

Charisma, however, must be taken in the context of early years provision. Indeed, an effective early years head should be charismatic (1.4a), but not at the expense of other people or the service provided. Charisma should help support good leadership, not hinder it. When the moment demands it, a charismatic leader will offer a different perspective or a creative idea, not the only perspective or the only idea. An effective early years manager will also have integrity (1.4b).

Elaine is the head of a local village pre-school. 'I try to create an atmosphere of excitement and energy, of optimism, communication and trust. I try not to be a sober and wet leader. As the head you are the figurehead for the pre-school, so if you come across as positive and energetic, full of good ideas, and welcoming, the community see the playgroup as a place that generates all of those things. The benefits of that can't be overstated. Your colleagues have faith in you and enjoy working with you. There are all kinds of benefits in this outside interest, not least financial ones. I don't take things too far though. "A full moon blanks out all the stars," as they say. I'm as involved and energetic as I need to be. Everyone is a leader of sorts at our pre-school.'

The outcomes of good charismatic leadership are many. They include excitement, involvement, optimism, vision, inspiration, innovation, as well as responsibility and accountability. Charismatic leaders are able to repackage complex ideas as straightforward messages and generate good communication. They involve others in their ideas and innovations, but they also involve others in the conception of these ideas and innovations. Charismatic leaders have the capacity to engage others and to spontaneously involve people in significant aspects of their leadership. These same people are drawn to what the leader is doing and what she has to say because she is charismatic and therefore engaging. An effective early years head, therefore, should be able to engage and involve others in ideas, innovations, goals and visions (1.4c).

'A lot of it boils down to respect,' says Elaine. 'A good leader is respected . . . and in turn she shows a lot of respect for her staff.' Indeed, mutual respect amongst staff is always a welcome commodity, regardless of the business. A good charismatic leader respects everyone she comes into contact with, children as well as staff and parents. Indeed, an effective early years head should command and offer respect (1.4d). 'Mind you, this sometimes takes a lot of persistence and the ability to argue things through in a knowledgeably and systematic way,' says Elaine (1.4e).

'As well as respect, I think motivation is really important. As I said, a good leader galvanizes you into action. The head I worked for who had no charisma just wasn't motivating. She would ask us to do things, but we didn't know why and she couldn't somehow convince us. There was a fundamental problem with communication. My second head, the woman on whom I have modelled myself as a leader, often didn't even need to tell us what to do, because she'd involved us in the earlier stages of her idea or decision. We all felt some degree of ownership of the setting and would happily perform above and beyond the call of duty when needed.' An effective early years head, therefore, should be able to motivate staff (1.4e).

Stem 1.4	Leaves 1.4a–1.4e

An effective early years leader or manager should...

1.4 Be a leader (continued on next page)	*1.4a Be charismatic (originating from the Greek word for gift, charisma is often characterized as comprising good leadership, the ability to command loyalty, and a natural tendency for being popular amongst peers)*
	1.4b Have integrity and justified confidence (this involves being honest, compassionate, and adhering to moral or artistic values and, in the process, ensuring that charisma does not exist in isolation but is coupled with good sense and good judgement)
	1.4c Be able to engage and involve others in ideas, innovations, goals and visions, and to compromise where relevant (this involves having sophisticated communication skills, requiring a high energy person to whom others are attentive)
	1.4d Command respect and offer respect (this involves being neither ingratiating nor difficult to please, ensuring that due praise is given and undue praise not, so that good practice is not devalued)
	1.4e Be able to motivate and persuade staff (this involves combining the ability to galvanize staff into action and lead them by persuasion and example with the ability to promote a philosophy of shared ownership of the setting)

List your targets	
Formulate an action plan	

Reflect on your capabilities and complete the boxes ...

What are your strengths?
Which areas need improvement?
What can you do to build on your strengths?
What do you need to do to improve your skills and
capabilities?

What are your strengths?
Which areas need improvement?
What can you do to build on your strengths?
What do you need to do to improve your skills and
capabilities?

What are your strengths?
Which areas need improvement?
What can you do to build on your strengths?
What do you need to do to improve your skills and
capabilities?

What are your strengths?
Which areas need improvement?
What can you do to build on your strengths?
What do you need to do to improve your skills and
capabilities?

What are your strengths?
Which areas need improvement?
What can you do to build on your strengths?
What do you need to do to improve your skills and
capabilities?

Stem 1.4 (cont.)	Leaf 1.4f

An effective early years leader or manager should . . .

1.4 *Be a leader* (continued from previous page)	1.4f *Persevere with understanding and developing the leadership role (this means that leaders need to work at enabling everyone to come to a clear understanding of the setting's current and future thinking and direction)*

List your targets	
Formulate an action plan	

Reflect on your capabilities and complete the boxes...

What are your strengths?
Which areas need improvement?
What can you do to build on your strengths?
What do you need to do to improve your skills and
capabilities?

Use this space for writing

Use this space for writing

Use this space for writing

Use this space for writing

Stem 1.5	Leaves 1.5a–1.5c

An effective early years leader or manager should...

1.5 Be flexible and versatile	1.5a View early years leadership as interchangeable, a situational phenomenon (that is, there is no set formula for running all settings which guarantees success: there is only good professional judgement, adaptability and flexibility)

	1.5b View change as a positive occurrence and respond confidently (this involves promoting a shared philosophy of change, being able to allay feelings of uncertainty, and provide informed support and time)

	1.5c Take risks based on clear understanding of the situation (this involves leaders pushing themselves and everyone that bit further from the basis of clear knowledge and understanding of early childhood care and education as it relates to the particular setting)

List your targets	
Formulate an action plan	

Reflect on your capabilities and complete the boxes...

What are your strengths?
Which areas need improvement?
What can you do to build on your strengths?
What do you need to do to improve your skills and
capabilities?

What are your strengths?
Which areas need improvement?
What can you do to build on your strengths?
What do you need to do to improve your skills and
capabilities?

Use this space for writing

Use this space for writing

Use this space for writing

Stem 1.6 Be knowledgeable

Cameo: Paulette

'There has been a marked change in the way early years professionals are expected to care and teach in recent years,' says Paulette. 'There has been a lot of emphasis on research and "evidence-informed practice". Professionals are not expected just to get on with caring and teaching, working by their instincts. Now, expectations are that they act intentionally and expertly, backing up their actions with theory and evidence.' She goes on. 'It is a heavy burden in many ways because early years work is still poorly paid, in my opinion, and is still not taken as seriously as it should be. For example, from one direction we are being told that we must be this and that, whilst from another our views are being ignored completely.'

Paulette is the head of a college day care unit. She believes that early years professionals need expert subject knowledge but is sympathetic to her staff for the lack of time, money and resources available for professional development. 'It is tough, yes. But there is still no excuse. Early years providers have a huge responsibility to society in caring for and teaching our youngest children. Pre-school is as important as school and the staff must be equally of high quality. The staff must, therefore, share this drive for professional self-improvement.'

One thing that Paulette does as the head of the setting is to ensure that she accommodates training courses within her budget, and that duties are relinquished so that staff are able to spend time developing themselves professionally. 'The staff are knowledgeable, all of them. It is, of course, essential that I share their knowledge. In meetings we often discuss issues relating to principles and theory and it would feel and look inadequate if I were not able to contribute.'

Paulette continues. 'Child development and psychology are particular interests of mine. I find it incredibly interesting; . . . it's great to be able to see what you're reading being put into action the next day!' All those working in early childhood know that child development is usually divided into five subsections: physical, social, emotional, linguistic and cognitive. A working knowledge of these five areas and how children perceive the world is essential for competent early years professionals. An effective early years head must have knowledge and understanding of child development and child psychology (1.6a).

'Closely linked to subject knowledge is the curriculum. Because there is only "Guidance", staff must also have a working knowledge of the broader curriculum, how different curricula operate, why they are important, their limitations and their advantages,' she acknowledges. 'Because of the National Curriculum, the focus is mainly on "what" is learnt in education rather than "how" it is learnt. This is different in the Early Years Foundation Stage, so my staff all have ideas about how children should learn as well as what they should learn . . . backed up with theory, of course!' An effective early years head, therefore, should have knowledge and understanding of curricula (1.6b).

One thing that effective managers have to know is their position in relation to local policy and legislation. What is the setting entitled to? What are the children entitled to? What regulations and policies must be followed? What are the legal rights of staff, children and parents? All these questions should be answerable if the head is conscientious enough and has a knowledge that extends beyond early years theory and continues into the realms of business management and law. An effective early years head, therefore, should have knowledge and understanding of related local policy (1.6c) and have knowledge and understanding of current legislation (1.6d).

'In any profession, knowledge is power,' says Paulette. 'It's the same in early years. In order to provide the best possible service for children and parents, the provider needs this type of power; ... the power to first determine what is right for the child and then secondly to resource and deliver it. The only way to ensure that this standard is kept up is if all staff are encouraged to be life-long learners and build on their current understanding and knowledge – just like children, really!'

Stem 1.6	Leaves 1.6a–1.6d

An effective early years leader or manager should . . .

1.6 Be knowledgeable and be an informational resource for staff	*1.6a Have knowledge and understanding of child development and child psychology (this involves not just knowing about these subjects but also using them to underpin professional practice in the setting)*
	1.6b Have knowledge and understanding of different curricula, both broad and specific national requirements (this involves being familiar with related documents such as the new EYFS* incorporating CGFS† and Birth–3 Matters)
	1.6c Have knowledge and understanding of related local policy and initiatives (this involves knowing about it, using it to underpin professional practice in the setting, and having named contacts for communication)
	1.6d Have knowledge and understanding of current legislation and national policy initiatives (this involves knowing your legal position through familiarity with legislation such as the Children Act 2004 and the Disability Discrimination Act 1995)

List your targets	
Formulate an action plan	

*Early Years Foundation Stage   † Curriculum Guidance for the Foundation Stage

Reflect on your capabilities and complete the boxes . . .

What are your strengths?
Which areas need improvement?
What can you do to build on your strengths?
What do you need to do to improve your skills and
capabilities?

What are your strengths?
Which areas need improvement?
What can you do to build on your strengths?
What do you need to do to improve your skills and
capabilities?

What are your strengths?
Which areas need improvement?
What can you do to build on your strengths?
What do you need to do to improve your skills and
capabilities?

What are your strengths?
Which areas need improvement?
What can you do to build on your strengths?
What do you need to do to improve your skills and
capabilities?

Use this space for writing

Stem 1.7 Understand the importance of shared values

Cameo: Rick

'Like-mindedness, that's what I promote in the nursery. Staff are not all the same, nor should they be. That they are like-minded does not, therefore, mean that they all share the same opinion; members of staff are not forced to think and feel in a particular way. What like-mindedness means, to me at least, is that everyone involved in the setting is in agreement as to what is important about the job – that they all have the same values and vision. Such things as equal opportunities, compassion, patience, partnerships with parents, the long-term future and achievement of the child, and providing a quality service, in terms of education and care. Like-mindedness means having shared values; working individually in a joint enterprise; working in your unique way to the same ends.'

Rick, the head of a maintained nursery, describes one of the key factors in successfully running an early years setting: cultivating shared values. As Rick says, 'A boat will not reach its destination if its crew are all rowing in opposite directions.' Similarly, an early years setting will not promote confident and capable children if mixed messages pervade the learning environment.

Clarity about what is right and desirable for the children and the setting may be the responsibility of the head. 'Our shared values are partly the result of working together for years, partly the product of numerous long meetings, and partly due to the commitment of all staff members to overcome their prejudices and professional flaws. I don't think I could express in words what our shared values are, nor do I expect any members of staff could, even though some of them are far more articulate than I am. We do, however, all have the same understanding ... a tacit understanding. We often take as our house motto the title of the recent DfES Circular, *Excellence and Enjoyment.*' There are numerous ways of cultivating shared values. One the most effective is to use meetings for the development of staff thinking as well as addressing important issues and delegating work, as Rick does. An effective early years head, therefore, should be able to generate shared values amongst staff within the setting (1.7).

When children encounter something for the first time they often look to others, namely adults or other children, for guidance on how to interpret and react to what is going on. This is called 'social referencing', and it is important that staff understand it as a moral responsibility they have to the children. Children's social referencing requires that staff have shared values they can impart, so that mixed messages are not transmitted within the setting and qualities such as empathy and compassion are developed. One thing that should be prized by everybody in the setting is equality of opportunity. Everyone should believe that all those involved in the setting are entitled to the same rights regardless of family, background, ethnicity, gender and religion. Indeed, since the coming into force of the Children Act in 1989 and the subsequent 2004 legislation (see DfES 2004a) and Green Paper *Every Child Matters* (DfES 2004b), this requirement is enshrined in law.

Stereotypes can be adopted by children from an early age. A stereotype can override the actual experiences of a child, leading them to believe that a particular group of people share certain (often negative) characteristics. To overcome this, children and staff need regular contact with groups in danger of being victimized by stereotyping, such as disabled people and those from different ethnic or racial backgrounds. 'We often have visitors from different cultural and religious backgrounds,' Rick says. 'We have posters on the walls, theme days, and use lots of stories to teach the children about different cultures and enhance their knowledge and understanding of other ethnic groups.' Closely linked to stereotyping is prejudice or 'pre-judgement'. An effective early years head should ensure that neither staff nor children develop negative or harmful values or traits, such as prejudice and stereotyping (1.7b, 1.7c, 1.7d).

As well as having goals for the future, staff should also have daily expectations of themselves. As well as a destination, staff should feel they have direction. This direction comes from the shared values of the setting. Knowing what to do in a given situation – feeling confident about knowing how to deal with a difficult child or parent in a way that is appropriate for them – comes from having clear shared values and a shared philosophy amongst staff. An effective early years head should ensure that both the direction and the destination of the setting are built into its organizational and philosophical framework (1.7c).

Having shared values depends on good communication: having a strong willingness to include and involve parents and staff is another. 'Values are not shared if the head sits in her office looking down on her staff, telling them constantly what they should do and how they should do it. Values are only "shared" if they have arisen organically from staff and management, through talking and reflecting on experience,' Rick states. 'Staff need to believe in what they're doing; they need to have ownership of it. If they have conflicting values and feel as though they are not valued, staff will be unhappy and ineffective as teachers and carers.' An effective early years manager should therefore ensure that all members of staff and all parents feel included and valued (1.7d).

Stem 1.7	**Leaves 1.7a–1.7d**

An effective early years leader or manager should . . .

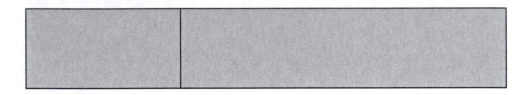

1.7 Understand the importance of shared values	1.7a Be able to generate shared values amongst staff within the setting (this involves knowing the staff well, having realistic ambitions for the setting, and being able to integrate them all to complementary effect)
	1.7b Ensure that neither staff nor children develop negative or harmful values or traits, such as prejudice and stereotyping (this involves giving them the opportunity to interact with minority cultures)
	1.7c Ensure that the culture, direction and destination of the setting are built into its organizational framework (this involves ensuring the awareness of both staff and parents, made possible through explicit communication)
	1.7d Ensure that all members of staff and all parents feel included and valued (this involves ensuring that all parties are involved and informed, their input is valued, and they have consequent feelings of ownership)

List your targets	
Formulate an action plan	

Reflect on your capabilities and complete the boxes ...

What are your strengths?
Which areas need improvement?
What can you do to build on your strengths?
What do you need to do to improve your skills and
capabilities?

What are your strengths?
Which areas need improvement?
What can you do to build on your strengths?
What do you need to do to improve your skills and
capabilities?

What are your strengths?
Which areas need improvement?
What can you do to build on your strengths?
What do you need to do to improve your skills and
capabilities?

What are your strengths?
Which areas need improvement?
What can you do to build on your strengths?
What do you need to do to improve your skills and
capabilities?

Use this space for writing

Stem 1.8 Understand how to lead and manage change

Cameo: Kathryn

'Change is one of life's few inevitabilities. Because of the growth of professionalism, which has particularly affected early years providers, leading change has become crucial to effective early years management. I try to be proactive rather than reactive when dealing with change, and I encourage my staff to see it as a positive phenomenon.'

Kathryn is the franchise manager of a private nursery. She has been in childcare since the late 1980s, so she remembers the introduction of the Children Act in 1989, which had a profound effect on the profession. 'There was a lot of resistance back then,' she says, 'and that was before change became a common occurrence.'

Resistance to change is as inevitable as change itself. Staff can feel threatened and anxious about their future, job security, mastery of the job and ability to meet new demands. This is to be expected, but an effective early years head should be able to allay these anxieties and encourage a positive philosophy towards change.

Kathryn is proactive when dealing with change. This means that she can take a step back, assess any new information that has come to her attention, discuss the possibility of change with her staff, then make a considered decision. 'At our centre we all share the same attitude to change ... it is inevitable, resisting it is counter-productive. ... We all encourage each other and always discuss outcomes. Nobody is ever kept in the dark and I keep everyone well informed. I trust the team and they trust me. They are all excellent, and everybody has confidence in themselves and their colleagues. Nobody worries that either their job or their "role" in the nursery will be affected.' Indeed, an effective early years head should have a positive attitude to change (1.8a) and be proactive rather than reactive to change (1.8b).

A key skill in effective change management is diagnosis. 'Obviously you learn from experience, but my ability to identify and even anticipate the need for change has improved greatly over the years. Sometimes change comes from outside the nursery, as an external force, but often the most effective changes you make are those that you put into motion yourself, those internal changes. I always keep my staff well informed and I keep up with social, economic and political developments. Small changes are often all that's needed to keep up standards and efficiency.' An effective early years head, as Kathryn says, must have the wisdom to identify the need for change from within and anticipate the demand for change from outside (1.8c).

The way change is implemented is crucial. It can be undertaken in large, unmanageable steps that disorientate staff, or in small manageable steps that involve all those concerned. 'When implementing change I use a method I got out of a textbook,' says Kathryn. 'It proposes implementing change in three stages. The first involves "unfreezing" the staff, which means making them more receptive to change, seeing it as an inevitable and positive process, and beginning to distance them from their old ways or perspectives. The next stage is change itself, its implementation. The last step is called "refreezing", which means stabilizing the change and making it the status quo. It is often a case of confidence rebuilding. The same applies to parents where possible. I always keep them informed and emphasize the positives involved in the change. Moreover, I try to have two approaches to change: one regarding the nursery, one the children. I try to keep the children's lives stable and predictable as far as possible, but I'm regularly trying to update and extend the nursery as a service provider.' An effective early years head, therefore, should implement relevant changes manageably whilst involving and reassuring staff and parents (1.8d).

Leading and managing change, like many areas of early years leadership, depends on good communication. Staff and parents should be kept well-informed. In this way, trust and confidence are generated and those who are involved, and those who will be affected, feel as though they have some ownership of it. Staff, especially, will resettle much quicker if they feel as if they were part of the process and had some degree of control over it. Strategies for dealing with change should be developed. The change that has just taken place can be seen as positive, inevitable, evolutionary, non-threatening and necessary, for example. Amongst other things, an effective early years manager should know how to resettle staff, parents and children following change (1.8e).

Rodd (2006: 183) identified eleven aspects of change that everyone should know about. She states that change:

1. is inevitable;
2. is necessary;
3. is a process;
4. occurs in individuals, organizations and societies;
5. can be anticipated and planned for;
6. is highly emotional and can cause tension and stress;
8. is resisted by many people;
9. can be adjusted to by individuals and groups with the support of a leader;
10. entails developmental growth in attitudes and skills, policies and procedures;
11. is best facilitated on the basis of diagnostic needs.

Such lists can facilitate leaders thinking about the needs of others during a process of change. Another example might be useful: one of the most important changes a child goes through is the transition from pre-school to school. Lyus (1998: 169–70) believes such transitions can be supported by the following means:

1. transferring relevant records about the child to the school;
2. arranging for the reception teacher to visit the pre-school setting;
3. arranging for the key worker to visit the school;
4. arranging for the child and parents to visit the school;
5. encouraging the child to read books about the school;
6. including school uniforms in the dressing-up box;
7. encouraging the receiving school to include role play about change;
8. ensuring the key worker talks to the child about the school.

Stem 1.8	Leaves 1.8a–1.8f

An effective early years leader or manager should...

1.8 Understand how to lead and manage change	1.8a Have a positive attitude to change and compromise (this involves encouraging staff to view change not as a problem but as an opportunity, and may involve combating the view of 'change for the sake of change' within education and care)
	1.8b Be proactive rather than reactive to change (this involves having a philosophical view of change, taking a step back, noting areas for improvement yourself, not pressing the panic button, and involving staff)
	1.8c Have the wisdom to identify the need for change from within and anticipate the demand for change from outside (this involves having diagnostic skills and being able to understand how to identify strengths and weaknesses and take remedial action)
	1.8d Implement relevant changes sensitively whilst involving and reassuring staff and parents (this involves suiting the pace of the change to the staff, communicating openly, and using SWOT – strengths, weaknesses, opportunities and threats – analysis)
	1.8e Know how to support staff, parents and children following change (this may involve using tried and tested procedures and models such as the three-stage unfreeze / change / refreeze method)
	1.8f Be aware of the effect that change, coming from the home or the setting, can have on children (this involves being sensitive to both prospective transitions, such as school, and possible transitions, such as divorce)

List your targets	
Formulate an action plan	

Reflect on your capabilities and complete the boxes...

What are your strengths?
Which areas need improvement?
What can you do to build on your strengths?
What do you need to do to improve your skills and
capabilities?

What are your strengths?
Which areas need improvement?
What can you do to build on your strengths?
What do you need to do to improve your skills and
capabilities?

What are your strengths?
Which areas need improvement?
What can you do to build on your strengths?
What do you need to do to improve your skills and
capabilities?

What are your strengths?
Which areas need improvement?
What can you do to build on your strengths?
What do you need to do to improve your skills and
capabilities?

What are your strengths?
Which areas need improvement?
What can you do to build on your strengths?
What do you need to do to improve your skills and
capabilities?

What are your strengths?
Which areas need improvement?
What can you do to build on your strengths?
What do you need to do to improve your skills and
capabilities?

Stem 1.9 Ensure that all relevant people are empowered

Cameo: Yafa

Yafa runs a small maintained nursery. She had been a primary school teacher, but chose to resign in order to take over the nursery. 'For some reason I was under the impression that running the nursery would be a piece of cake,' she recalls; 'a nice break from primary teaching. Needless to say, I was completely wrong!'

'I took over the nursery in 2000. The head before me was a bit of a dinosaur, using mainly primary school methods – she was a real disciplinarian. The teachers weren't given any autonomy or freedom, which didn't have a particularly positive effect on their morale. Teachers feel restrained enough by procedures like OfSTED inspections, but limiting the decisions they can make, and keeping them in the dark with regard to things such as policy just demotivates them. I think it was easier for me to go from teacher to head because I was more aware of what my colleagues wanted and needed. In this way, I empowered them immediately by making those changes.'

Yafa used her own experience of being stifled by poor management as the basis for becoming a better head herself. Empowerment is undoubtedly a fashionable concept in business management, but it is more than just a fanciful term for delegation. It incorporates all kinds of important ideas, such as co-operation, participation, involvement, partnership and ownership. The basic premise is that the best possible working environment is one in which everyone has a measure of responsibility and the power to make their own decisions. An effective head should operate a system of empowerment (1.9), in which children, staff and parents feel enabled, valued, able to voice their opinions, and empathic to the setting and its practices. Parents in the most effective settings are particularly valued as partners, experts and parallel educators (Hunt and Robson 1999).

Adults (staff and parents in particular) are not the only prospective beneficiaries of empowerment. Children can be empowered too. In New Zealand, early years practitioners approach each child as a unique individual, using as their starting point the individual skills, knowledge and experiences of that child, through the Te Whaariki curriculum (Guild *et al.* 1998). In this way they have a foundation of independence on which to build. Te Whaariki, Maori for 'woven mat', effectively communicates the idea that early years education has many 'threads' and aims to build a platform for the child to stand on in later life.

Similarly, in Reggio Emilia in Italy, children are encouraged to have some control over their learning and their learning environment (Edwards *et al.* 1998). The idea of empowering children, therefore, is one of the key concepts that underpins a number of cutting-edge early years practices. Children should feel enabled and in control of their learning and their environment. They should understand the activities they engage in as instances of play rather than work. An effective early years head, therefore, should empower children (1.9a). Indeed, it is every early years practitioner's responsibility to ensure that each child reaches his or her potential.

Empowering children may be the result of empowering staff, of giving them the power to make 'expert' decisions about the working environment, the curriculum and the child. Like all good cultural changes, empowerment has a knock-on effect. As well as the children, the staff should feel enabled and in control of their teaching, having a strong sense of ownership of the areas of the setting in which they operate. 'When I moved from primary to nursery leadership, I made sure I took with me the principle of empowerment. In essence it is all about teamwork and trust. Mind you, you do have to have brilliant staff whom you trust, otherwise you want to do all the work yourself and want to know exactly what everyone is doing all the time,' Yafa explains. An effective early years head should empower staff (1.9b).

As well as children and staff, an effective early years head should also empower parents and understand the multiple roles and responsibilities they have towards the child (1.9c). The parents are the child's first and most influential educators and have many other roles to adopt, including supporter, champion and decision maker. Parents can be empowered in the same way as staff, by keeping them involved and informed so that they share a sense of ownership of the setting, and by ensuring that their voices are heard so that they feel knowledgeable, informed and involved in their child's care and education.

Stem 1.9	**Leaves 1.9a–1.9c**

An effective early years leader or manager should . . .

1.9 Ensure that all relevant people are empowered and enabled	*1.9a Empower and enable children (this involves ensuring that all children feel enabled and, where possible, in control of their learning, as well as in helping them reach appropriate levels of confidence and competence)*

	1.9b Empower and enable staff (this involves ensuring that all staff feel enabled and, where possible, in control of their practice, as well as in helping them reach appropriate levels of confidence and competence)

	1.9c Empower and enable parents and understand the multiple roles and responsibilities they have towards their child(ren) (this involves encouraging parents to be teachers, supporters, advocates and decision makers for the child)

List your targets	
Formulate an action plan	

Reflect on your capabilities and complete the boxes...

What are your strengths?
Which areas need improvement?
What can you do to build on your strengths?
What do you need to do to improve your skills and
capabilities?

What are your strengths?
Which areas need improvement?
What can you do to build on your strengths?
What do you need to do to improve your skills and
capabilities?

What are your strengths?
Which areas need improvement?
What can you do to build on your strengths?
What do you need to do to improve your skills and
capabilities?

Use this space for writing

Use this space for writing

Stem 1.10 Be a culture setter

Cameo: Gene

'Being manager of a day nursery is completely different from how I imagined it,' says Gene, a head who is quite new to the profession. 'It's about being in control, but not in the way that I ever imagined. It seems to me that what is important is not necessarily having a controlling influence over the people within the setting, though ideally you would have this too. No, what is important from my experience is that you have the ability to influence the culture of the setting. If you have worked at developing a culture in which the management work closely with the staff, and in which children have fun but learn to be polite and considerate, then the need for direct control over them is far less, if you see what I mean.'

Indeed, being able to recognize and influence the atmosphere or ethos of the setting is central to managing it well, as Gene professes. A manager should be sensitive to the 'feeling' a setting has; they should have an awareness of how the people within the place truly feel about themselves and one another, and about their work. Some managers either turn a blind eye to what they fear is discontent amongst staff, or simply do not have the 'penetrating vision' to look beneath fake smiles and enthusiasm. Numerous methods, however, can be employed to ascertain 'inside' information about the ethos and culture of the setting under your management: anonymous questionnaires, meetings styled as open forums, the promotion of a culture of staff honesty, and many others. An effective early years head should know how to create an ethos that is appropriate for the setting (1.10a).

Having the ability to influence the culture of your environment is both a learnt and an intrinsic skill. Where natural ability is lacking there are means to improve one's awareness of organizational culture. 'I've taken a few courses on things like human resource management and management techniques, all different in length,' says Gene. 'I'm not naturally one of those people who are "tuned in" to others, I would say. But this is easily compensated. As I said, I've taken short courses to increase my awareness, and I don't try to pretend that as head I'm infallible. I think the staff feel comfortable talking to me about anything and we talk about ourselves as a team and as a cultural setting all the time in meetings.' Indeed, an effective early years head should understand the culture of organizations specifically and universally (1.10b).

'"Lead by example", as always, is the best approach to take in early years management,' Gene claims. 'You have to be a model of professionalism and epitomize the culture and spirit of the setting.' The manager should not stand outside of the team. The idea of synergy – of the whole being greater than the sum of the parts – is central to the successful running of any organization. Therefore, the staff team should be greater than the individuals who compose it. 'One way of ensuring that we work well as a team is by concentrating on what staff can do, not what they can't.' This is usually called the 'constructivist approach' and describes early years education in which carers build on what children know and can do, rather than 'filling the gaps' with what others deem important. This approach, however, is also effective amongst staff, utilizing their unique expertises. An effective early years head, therefore, should cultivate and represent the defining spirit of the setting (1.10c).

Although a well-managed setting will have a positive and enabling atmosphere, it is always good practice for staff to be able to articulate what exactly it is that makes the setting so good (or indeed what needs changing) (see Drury *et al.* 2000). This allows everyone involved in its running to be clear about what is valued and what contributes to making the ethos and appropriate culture of the setting. If one can isolate what are strengths and weaknesses, you can promote one and change the other. An effective head should therefore ensure that values are defined within the setting (1.10d) so that they are open to continual scrutiny and change.

Stem 1.10	**Leaves 1.10a–1.10d**

An effective early years leader or manager should...

1.10 Earn status and rank as a culture setter	*1.10a Know how to create an ethos appropriate for the setting (this involves being receptive to both the atmosphere of the setting and the attitude of the staff and then transforming them into the 'culture')*

	1.10b Understand the culture of organizations specifically and universally (this involves being able to determine what is good practice for settings in general and what is good practice for the setting in particular)

	1.10c Cultivate and represent the defining essence of the setting (this involves being influential, leading by example and being a transformational leader who 'transforms' values and beliefs into ethos and culture)

	1.10d Ensure that values and ethics are identified and defined within the setting (this may involve communicating values explicitly and physically through documents such as mission statements, as well as ensuring staff like-mindedness)

List your targets	
Formulate an action plan	

Reflect on your capabilities and complete the boxes . . .

What are your strengths?
Which areas need improvement?
What can you do to build on your strengths?
What do you need to do to improve your skills and
capabilities?

What are your strengths?
Which areas need improvement?
What can you do to build on your strengths?
What do you need to do to improve your skills and
capabilities?

What are your strengths?
Which areas need improvement?
What can you do to build on your strengths?
What do you need to do to improve your skills and
capabilities?

What are your strengths?
Which areas need improvement?
What can you do to build on your strengths?
What do you need to do to improve your skills and
capabilities?

Use this space for writing

4 The Management Skills branch

Introduction

There is more to running an early years setting than being a visionary and inspirational leader, vital as these qualities are. An effective early years head would, ideally, have leadership qualities and management skills in equal measure. Management has a wealth of varied literature to support it, albeit generic rather than specific, but rarely, as we have seen, is the literature aimed at the early years. However, management skills are arguably more 'learnable' than those related to leadership, though natural aptitude still features. As O'Sullivan (2003: 5) emphasizes: 'Management is a combination of theory and practice that is designed to ensure that the work of an organisation is developed, supported and guided by an individual or team so as to effectively meet the organisation's purposes.'

As an example, human resource management is partly about being able to deal with people sensitively. It is also about being familiar and confident with procedures and models of doing things, such as organizing staff, recruiting them, appraising them, monitoring and supporting them, and offering professional development opportunities. Taking this last item as an example, an effective early years head must understand both people (such as the professional development needs of each staff member) and procedures (such as how to go about securing the funding and organizing the time to offer professional development opportunities). Whereas leadership is about thinking 'outside the box' without the support of any specific guidelines, management is about being able to function well 'inside the box'. It is about doing the best for the setting within the given parameters (Collins 2001; Ebbeck and Waninganayake 2002) and is based on the 'principle of continuous improvement' (O'Sullivan 2003: 129).

As well as human resource management and the development of teamworking (2.1), curriculum management (2.2) is central to the role of an early years head. As in leadership, knowledge is of high value, but the conditions are different. A major part of human resource management is working effectively as a team leader and encouraging teamwork of the highest quality within the staff (Bartholomew 1996; Kydd *et al.* 2003). The effective curriculum leader perceives external involvement and influence such as government circulars as providing a scaffold from which to expand, not as a straitjacket (2.3, 2.4, 2.5).

There is a wealth of different management skills important in the early years, the major ones of which are communication and teamwork: amongst staff, with parents, with the community, and of course with children. This means understanding the strengths of multi- and bilingual children and communities and working with them effectively to celebrate diversity (see, for example, Siraj-Blatchford and Clarke 2000; Baker 2001). An effective head will confidently and knowledgeably lobby local officials and government representatives, and stay abreast of national/local news and related policies and directives (2.3–2.5) as well as being knowledgeable about aspects of early childhood at national and global level, for instance current research and its potential impact at setting, local and national level (2.5b, 2.5e).

Of paramount importance is the thinking behind, and actions involved, in decision making (2.6). Early years heads, far more so than other managers and leaders of small businesses, are responsible for lively, impressionable, vulnerable and intelligent young people – the children. In fact, the head's role eclipses all but those in the largest organizations in relation to the sheer numbers of people for whom they are responsible. Most leaders deal mainly with staff – and maybe products. Hardly ever are they responsible for so many people and certainly not such young children. As is evident, a single decision has great consequences for many individuals (Crawford 2003).

Like all managers, the early years head should be adept at planning and strategy making (2.7). Being able to plan and organize effectively with so many people to consider, in both the short and the long term, and ensuring that everyone is appropriately informed of every significant development as well, is a huge talent; a management skill indeed (Bell 2002).

As well as managing human resources and being able to work effectively with people, an effective early years head is adept at the implementation and monitoring of ideas and putting them into practice as well as understanding inspection and compliance issues (2.8). Being able to undertake other administrative tasks such as ensuring effective and efficient admission and registration procedures (2.9) and dealing with the budget, organizing resources and ensuring that everything is legally sound, as well as safe and stimulating, constitute many challenging tasks (2.10). An effective early years head is a scientist and mathematician as well as an artist; is as comfortable with people as the subject or object of management as they are with materials; is as comfortable doing something as they are thinking about and developing it, and far more.

The fewer cameos in this section reflect the fact that the skills of management appear, as anticipated in the Introduction, to be far easier to understand and carry out than the more esoteric leadership and attitudinal components.

Stem 2.1	**Leaves 2.1a–2.1e**

An effective early years leader or manager should...

2.1 Ensure effective human resource management and administration (continued on next page)	*2.1a Be a competent organizer and know how to assign staff, ensuring that they are well matched to their tasks (this may involve eliciting individual strengths of staff and ensuring staff profiles match school development plans)*

	2.1b Be an effective recruiter and retainer of staff, ensuring that staff numbers are optimum (this involves identifying suitable staff and then ensuring that they feel valued and supported once recruited)

	2.1c Be an effective appraiser of staff, being encouraging, supportive, firm and constructively critical where necessary (this involves setting achievable individual goals for staff and having professional development targets)

	2.1d Be an effective motivator and supporter of staff, giving them energy and instilling their work with meaning and value (this involves leading by example, working with energy and having a sense of purpose)

	2.1e Ensure that staff have appropriate professional development opportunities (this involves making provision for personal development and research, providing financial support and relinquishing duties)

List your targets	
Formulate an action plan	

Reflect on your capabilities and complete the boxes . . .

What are your strengths?
Which areas need improvement?
What can you do to build on your strengths?
What do you need to do to improve your skills and
capabilities?

What are your strengths?
Which areas need improvement?
What can you do to build on your strengths?
What do you need to do to improve your skills and
capabilities?

What are your strengths?
Which areas need improvement?
What can you do to build on your strengths?
What do you need to do to improve your skills and
capabilities?

What are your strengths?
Which areas need improvement?
What can you do to build on your strengths?
What do you need to do to improve your skills and
capabilities?

What are your strengths?
Which areas need improvement?
What can you do to build on your strengths?
What do you need to do to improve your skills and
capabilities?

Stem 2.1 (cont.)	Leaves 2.1f–2.1j

An effective early years leader or manager should...

2.1 Ensure effective human resource management and administration (continued from previous page)	**2.1f** Ensure good working relations and networking with staff and amongst staff *(this involves attaining a suitable balance between having a formal and an informal environment, between business and pleasure, and work and play)*

	2.1g Ensure positive relations with parents and the community and encourage staff to do the same *(this involves marketing the setting to the local community and involving and informing parents where possible)*

	2.1h Ensure appropriate authority is maintained whilst offering democratic approaches to others *(this involves being able to exercise an enabling rather than a restricting amount of control over staff when necessary)*

	2.1i Ensure staff feel included and responsible, optimizing their performance and well-being *(this involves treating all staff as important individuals, as a team, that is, but not one made up of identical persons)*

	2.1j Ensure good practice is recognized and poor practice is moderated *(this involves having to approach staff to confront poor practice, provide support and training where necessary and harness good practice)*

List your targets	
Formulate an action plan	

Reflect on your capabilities and complete the boxes...

What are your strengths?
Which areas need improvement?
What can you do to build on your strengths?
What do you need to do to improve your skills and
capabilities?

What are your strengths?
Which areas need improvement?
What can you do to build on your strengths?
What do you need to do to improve your skills and
capabilities?

What are your strengths?
Which areas need improvement?
What can you do to build on your strengths?
What do you need to do to improve your skills and
capabilities?

What are your strengths?
Which areas need improvement?
What can you do to build on your strengths?
What do you need to do to improve your skills and
capabilities?

What are your strengths?
Which areas need improvement?
What can you do to build on your strengths?
What do you need to do to improve your skills and
capabilities?

Stem 2.2	Leaves 2.2a–2.2e

An effective early years leader or manager should . . .

2.2 Ensure effective curriculum management	*2.2a Ensure effective and appropriate curriculum planning (this involves having an in-depth knowledge of curricula and being a competent planner, as well as being familiar with each group, child and carer)*

	2.2b Ensure effective and appropriate curriculum implementation (this involves bringing the curriculum to life through suitable activities and monitoring the way both staff and children respond to it)

	2.2c Ensure effective and appropriate curriculum evaluation (this may involve having a systematic model for assessing the effectiveness of curricular activities, as well as gauging the reaction of the staff)

	2.2d Manage and lead effective and appropriate curriculum change (this involves first being able to suitably review and evaluate the curriculum, then being able to isolate the problem and implement the change needed)

	2.2e Promote consistent and appropriate daily curriculum routines for staff and children (this involves skill at short-term planning, good communication with staff, and knowledge of relevant curricula and children)

List your targets	
Formulate an action plan	

Reflect on your capabilities and complete the boxes...

What are your strengths?
Which areas need improvement?
What can you do to build on your strengths?
What do you need to do to improve your skills and
capabilities?

What are your strengths?
Which areas need improvement?
What can you do to build on your strengths?
What do you need to do to improve your skills and
capabilities?

What are your strengths?
Which areas need improvement?
What can you do to build on your strengths?
What do you need to do to improve your skills and
capabilities?

What are your strengths?
Which areas need improvement?
What can you do to build on your strengths?
What do you need to do to improve your skills and
capabilities?

What are your strengths?
Which areas need improvement?
What can you do to build on your strengths?
What do you need to do to improve your skills and
capabilities?

Stems 2.3–2.5 Ensure effective interaction, involvement and intervention at all levels

Cameo: Nadine

Nadine is the head of a large day care centre. She feels strongly about the involvement of parents and has remained positive about the political attention that her profession has received in recent years. 'The secret of a good day care centre, in my opinion, is to involve, as much as you possibly can, all of the interested parties.'

Nadine used to feel differently towards parents. 'A few years ago there was a lot of emphasis on "shared child rearing" between staff and parents,' Nadine recalls. 'Although this seems to be common sense, personally I had never before conceptualized the relationship between staff and parents as one of partnership. That revelation represented a big shift in my personal philosophy.' An effective early years head must understand the relationship between parents and staff as one of partnership and mutual benefit (2.3a, 2.4a, 2.5a).

'A day care centre', Nadine adds, 'does not only have an educational responsibility to the children it cares for, it also has a responsibility to the parents of those children. To minimize tension and maximize harmony between the centre and the home, early years providers should educate and inform parents as well as children ... but also be prepared to learn from parents.'

Disseminating accurate information to the appropriate people is a key skill in early years management, and keeping staff and parents informed is essential. 'Good communication and dissemination of information ensures that the two agents in the system run in tandem, rather than in conflict with each other.' An effective early years head, as Nadine advocates, should fulfil the responsibility of supporting the education of parents as well as children (2.3b) and undertake good two-way communication to ensure parity of approach and philosophy between staff and parents (2.3c).

'I think that a number of the staff would say that dealing with parents is the most difficult part of their job. ... But when the head keeps parents, as well as staff, informed about policy and practice, so that nobody is left in the dark, half the battle is won. Both parents and staff are experts within different areas of expertise. This is a realization that every head must come to.' An effective early years head should recognize and utilize the different but complementary expertise of staff and parents (2.3d).

'Effective involvement with parents is also good for the esteem of the Centre,' says Nadine. 'Since parents have been more involved, our reputation has certainly increased in relation to their confidence in us and our confidence in them. There is also the added bonus of their growing appreciation for our professionalism.' Like Nadine, all effective early years heads should appreciate that parents play a key role in determining the level of professional recognition received by the early years profession (2.3e).

'The importance of the Centre to the community cannot be underestimated,' Nadine continues. 'If school is the foundation of society, the place where standards and values are set, then pre-school services must be just as important, and just as influential in determining the future of our society.'

Early years provision has a huge responsibility to society in ensuring that children will be cared for and educated appropriately not only to their current individual and collective needs but also in relation to their role as citizens now and in the future. The importance of what the profession does is gaining greater recognition as more and more research shows the value, impact and long-term benefits of early education (Sylva *et al.* 2004). An effective early years head must understand the relationship of the child to the local and national community (2.4a, 2.5a).

In recent years, early years has increasingly become the focus of public and media attention, moving the profession much more into a political arena. The belief that children should not be mixed with politics has changed, and now the profession needs a political voice so that the government is aware of its needs and understands the way it operates. 'My job has broadened over the years,' Nadine says. 'It used to be quite an insular profession, but now it is the responsibility of every early years head to keep up with local and government policy and related issues that may have an impact upon the setting and/or the profession' (2.4b, 2.5b).

'I don't know my local member of parliament very well, but I do know who he is, and I do have the means to contact him if the need arose. I think it is every head's responsibility to know something about the political scene and who operates it at local and national level,' Nadine proposes (2.4c, 2.5c). 'You should be willing and able to lobby if push comes to shove.'

In order for the government to make informed changes to the early years profession, they need to be well-informed. It is the collective responsibility of early years heads to ensure that the right people are provided with relevant information in order to make informed policies. There are numerous groups competing for the attention of the government; numerous voices, therefore, to which the government should listen. Voices from the early years profession need to be heard. Early years heads, therefore, should attempt to raise the profile of the profession within the local and national community (2.4d, 2.5d).

'One tip for keeping on top of legislation and policy', says Nadine, 'is to keep everything organized. That way you can reference easily. I have a room, a kind of archive, where I keep all important documents. These are available to anyone involved, including staff, parents, myself, and any other interested party.' An organized early years head, therefore, would hold all relevant local and government legislative documents in a suitable place that is accessible for others (2.4e, 2.5f). In sum, it is the responsibility of the head to market the setting and/or the profession effectively to the local community (2.4f).

Stem 2.3	Leaves 2.3a–2.3e

An effective early years leader or manager should . . .

2.3 Ensure effective interaction, involvement and intervention at setting level	*2.3a Understand the relationship between parents and staff as one of partnership and mutual benefit (this involves synchronizing the setting and the home so that each benefits and complements the other)*

	2.3b Fulfil the responsibility of supporting the education of parents as well as children (this involves keeping parents regularly informed and involved, offering, as experts, advice on children and childcare)

	2.3c Undertake good two-way communication to ensure parity of approach and philosophy between staff and parents (this involves allowing time and devising ways for staff and parents to have regular dialogues)

	2.3d Recognize and utilize the different but complementary expertise of differentially trained staff and of parents (this involves encouraging different approaches from staff and parents where necessary)

	2.3e Appreciate that parents have a key role in determining the level of professional recognition received by the setting and the early years profession (that is, what is marketed well to parents will have a ripple effect)

List your targets	
Formulate an action plan	

Reflect on your capabilities and complete the boxes ...

What are your strengths?
Which areas need improvement?
What can you do to build on your strengths?
What do you need to do to improve your skills and
capabilities?

What are your strengths?
Which areas need improvement?
What can you do to build on your strengths?
What do you need to do to improve your skills and
capabilities?

What are your strengths?
Which areas need improvement?
What can you do to build on your strengths?
What do you need to do to improve your skills and
capabilities?

What are your strengths?
Which areas need improvement?
What can you do to build on your strengths?
What do you need to do to improve your skills and
capabilities?

What are your strengths?
Which areas need improvement?
What can you do to build on your strengths?
What do you need to do to improve your skills and
capabilities?

Stem 2.4	Leaves 2.4a–2.4f

An effective early years leader or manager should...

2.4 Ensure effective interaction, involvement and intervention at local level	2.4a Understand the relationship of the child to the local community and, for example, its range of ethnic groups and languages (this involves understanding children as 'products' of their family, residential area, local culture, economic background, experience and religion)	→
	2.4b Stay abreast of local policy and related issues that may have an impact upon the setting and/or the profession (this involves being proactive and reading, disseminating and storing the relevant material)	→
	2.4c Know how the political scene operates and who is involved at local level (this may involve marketing the setting to the relevant people and lobbying when necessary, as well as keeping abreast of local news)	→
	2.4d Raise the profile of the setting and/or the profession within the local community (this may involve networking and liaising with connected people, establishing the setting within the community)	→
	2.4e Store all relevant local documents in a suitable location so as to be accessible for others (this involves being organized, tidy, well-informed and able to make information easily available to others)	→
	2.4f Market the setting and/or the profession effectively to the local community (this involves having a website, organizing events and fundraisers, distributing flyers and putting articles in local papers)	→

List your targets	
Formulate an action plan	

Reflect on your capabilities and complete the boxes . . .

What are your strengths?
Which areas need improvement?
What can you do to build on your strengths?
What do you need to do to improve your skills and
capabilities?

What are your strengths?
Which areas need improvement?
What can you do to build on your strengths?
What do you need to do to improve your skills and
capabilities?

What are your strengths?
Which areas need improvement?
What can you do to build on your strengths?
What do you need to do to improve your skills and
capabilities?

What are your strengths?
Which areas need improvement?
What can you do to build on your strengths?
What do you need to do to improve your skills and
capabilities?

What are your strengths?
Which areas need improvement?
What can you do to build on your strengths?
What do you need to do to improve your skills and
capabilities?

What are your strengths?
Which areas need improvement?
What can you do to build on your strengths?
What do you need to do to improve your skills and
capabilities?

Stem 2.5	Leaves 2.5a–2.5f

An effective early years leader or manager should . . .

2.5 Ensure effective interaction, involvement and intervention at national and international level	2.5a Understand the relationship of the child to the national/international community (this involves understanding children as products of society, especially of cultural forces such as the mass media, as well as of local and family culture)
	2.5b Stay abreast of government policy, research and related issues that may have an impact upon the setting and/or the profession (this involves being proactive, keeping abreast of national news and critically reflecting)
	2.5c Know how the political scene operates and who is involved at national level (this may involve marketing the setting to the wider community and establishing connections with the politically mobile – being visible)
	2.5d Endeavour to raise the profile of the setting and/or the profession within the national/international community (this may involve networking and liaising with connected people, establishing the setting within the community)
	2.5e Keep abreast of national/international research which can inform practice and thinking (this means making time to locate sources of information, e.g. early years journals, to read them and to consider what the research means to leadership practices)

List your targets	
Formulate an action plan	

Reflect on your capabilities and complete the boxes ...

What are your strengths?
Which areas need improvement?
What can you do to build on your strengths?
What do you need to do to improve your skills and
capabilities?

What are your strengths?
Which areas need improvement?
What can you do to build on your strengths?
What do you need to do to improve your skills and
capabilities?

What are your strengths?
Which areas need improvement?
What can you do to build on your strengths?
What do you need to do to improve your skills and
capabilities?

What are your strengths?
Which areas need improvement?
What can you do to build on your strengths?
What do you need to do to improve your skills and
capabilities?

What are your strengths?
Which areas need improvement?
What can you do to build on your strengths?
What do you need to do to improve your skills and
capabilities?

Use this space for writing

Stem 2.6 Ensure effective decision making

Cameo: Sally

Sally is the head of a local village nursery. 'I've never been the most decisive person,' she claims, 'but I've learnt over the years that being decisive isn't necessarily a good thing when it comes to management. Some heads can be too impulsive. Sometimes I have to make decisions on my own. Often, however, I enlist the help of my staff.'

There are numerous different types of decision making, each with a different level of group involvement. There are decisions made by a head on her own, decisions delegated by the head to an 'expert' member of staff, decisions made through majority group vote, and those discussed in a group with the final decision resting with the head. An awareness of these different approaches is important in management. An effective early years head should therefore ensure appropriate delegation of responsibilities for making decisions (2.6a) and ensure that the person to whom a task is delegated understands its parameters and his/her responsibilities (2.6b).

'I have a number of friends who are early years heads. They tend to bypass the whole democratic process when it comes to decision making, and then they moan about parents and staff criticizing them and the lack of support they get. ... I try to involve people whenever possible and I always inform my staff of any big decision I've made. This way I'm not more accountable and less open to criticism. People tend to be a lot more patient and supportive of decisions when you involve them and inform them.' An effective early years head should therefore make decisions explicit and inclusive where possible so that others have confidence in them (2.6c).

'One thing that I've personally found useful as a basis for making decisions is our mission statement. We have a couple of A4 sides that state what the nursery is about, what we believe in, what we represent, how we would like the nursery to be and what our ultimate aims are. If you have a clear idea of these things, of knowing which direction you want to be going in and what your final destination would ideally be, then you can make decisions in line with this. You can think to yourself, will this decision keep us going in the direction we have a shared belief in, or will that one?' As Sally says, an effective early years head should make decisions based on the vision of the setting, its direction and its destination (2.6d).

Below is a useful acronym to making a decision that is sensible, accountable, explicit and inclusive:

D	Define	–	the situation or goal
E	Establish	–	the contributing factors
C	Choose	–	which decisions might be made
I	Investigate	–	and evaluate the choices
S	Select	–	the best choice of decision
I	Implement	–	and carry out best choice
O	Organize	–	and be open, informing others of choice(s)
N	Negotiate	–	relevant choice(s)

Stem 2.6	Leaves 2.6a–2.6d

An effective early years leader or manager should…

2.6 Ensure effective decision making	2.6a Ensure appropriate delegation of responsibilities for making decisions (this involves knowing who is the expert on what amongst staff, as well as having the support of decision-making bodies such as committees)

	2.6b Delegate with responsibility; ensure that the people to whom a task is delegated understand its parameters and their responsibilities (this means that, once delegated, tasks should be seen to completion by the individual, with scheduled feedback on progress)

	2.6c Make decisions explicit and inclusive where possible so that others have confidence in them (this involves ensuring that staff and parents are always appropriately informed and involved)

	2.6d Make decisions based on the vision of the setting, its direction and its destination (this involves having shared philosophies and ambitions for the setting that are appropriate, explicit and referable)

List your targets	
Formulate an action plan	

Reflect on your capabilities and complete the boxes...

What are your strengths?
Which areas need improvement?
What can you do to build on your strengths?
What do you need to do to improve your skills and capabilities?

What are your strengths?
Which areas need improvement?
What can you do to build on your strengths?
What do you need to do to improve your skills and capabilities?

What are your strengths?
Which areas need improvement?
What can you do to build on your strengths?
What do you need to do to improve your skills and capabilities?

What are your strengths?
Which areas need improvement?
What can you do to build on your strengths?
What do you need to do to improve your skills and capabilities?

Use this space for writing

Stem 2.7	**Leaves 2.7a–2.7d**

An effective early years leader or manager should...

2.7 Ensure effective planning and strategy making	**2.7a** Be adept at short-term planning to support the smooth running of the setting on a daily basis (this involves having excellent administrative skills and being familiar with every child, carer and curriculum)
	2.7b Be adept at long-term planning to ensure fulfilment of the vision of the future of the setting (this involves having excellent managerial skills such as accounting, budgeting, resourcing and lobbying)
	2.7c Understand the value of curriculum planning and be adept at undertaking this for the benefit of both children and staff (this involves ensuring that all persons have continuity and quality in their daily lives)
	2.7d Ensure that the curriculum provides continuity between the home and the setting and between the setting and the school (this involves careful planning and good communications with other relevant settings)

List your targets	
Formulate an action plan	

Reflect on your capabilities and complete the boxes . . .

What are your strengths?
Which areas need improvement?
What can you do to build on your strengths?
What do you need to do to improve your skills and
capabilities?

What are your strengths?
Which areas need improvement?
What can you do to build on your strengths?
What do you need to do to improve your skills and
capabilities?

What are your strengths?
Which areas need improvement?
What can you do to build on your strengths?
What do you need to do to improve your skills and
capabilities?

What are your strengths?
Which areas need improvement?
What can you do to build on your strengths?
What do you need to do to improve your skills and
capabilities?

Use this space for writing

Stem 2.8 Ensure effective implementation and monitoring of ideas

Cameo: Patti

Patti is director of an early excellence centre which has undergone rapid expansion in the past few years. 'The process has been traumatic for everyone and there are many occasions on which the multi-disciplinary management team has just not managed to implement our ideas and carry all the staff with us. Staff seem to have been suffering from "initiative fatigue" and some have withdrawn into their own teaching area. Even some of the parents have showed signs of concern that they don't fully understand what is going on.' Patti and the staff had previously discussed the many changes that were likely because of the designation of the nursery as an Early Excellence Centre and made extensive plans to be implemented over a period of two terms. She decides that drastic measures are needed and plans a whole staff development day at a local hotel for the purpose of cementing staff relationships and getting them to review the plans they previously made together and find ways of implementing them efficiently and effectively (2.8a). 'My aim is to treat them to an enjoyable "groupthink" day – they'll be fed and watered royally – but then ensure that they give 100 per cent commitment to the plans made and overcome some of the psychological barriers they seem to have erected.'

It is vital that once efficient, team-inspired plans are made they are seen through and that staff are all committed to ensuring a successful outcome in the agreed timescale, even if that outcome is simply the beginning of many. Change as far-reaching as that involved in the redesignation of a centre can be harrowing for everyone involved. Trying to keep the centre running to everyone's satisfaction requires extensive managerial skills from the head, one of which is knowing how to get the best out of the staff and avoid any personality clashes likely to occur when staff feel that their particular responsibility or status is being usurped. Patti reported on the outcome of the away-day: 'It took over an hour to get all the staff on the same wavelength, but they quickly realized that they all wanted the changes as we'd originally agreed and the rest of the day was then spent on making decisions about how each person could best contribute to delivering and implementing our overall plan.'

Not only do staff need to be committed in this way, but they need to be involved in monitoring any necessary deviations from the original plans – for example, because of new curriculum requirements. Each member of staff should feel able to offer new, well conceived ideas for both the implementation and the monitoring and evaluation of the ensuing practice (2.8b). Patti ensured that each member of staff's plans for involvement in the changes were incorporated into their annual appraisal documents so that she had the chance to discuss each one's role, thinking and attitudes personally and professionally. 'I want to make everyone realize that I care about the new practices but also that I respect their views and ideas and that we are all pulling together,' says Patti. 'I also feel it's important to delegate with responsibility – it's no good if someone agrees to do a job and then I or someone else keeps interfering, however much we may want to. Staff know that, once we've agreed a responsibility for them, they report back to me or the senior management team at given points in the year to report on progress and share thoughts.'

Over the next few months, Patti's staff met in small groups, each of which had agreed at the away-day to monitor the changes. One representative then met with the senior management team who, in turn, analysed the effect of the different procedures which had been implemented in relation to the whole. Often this entailed analysing and evaluating particular practices to assess whether they had been successful (2.8c). Patti explains: 'It was really wonderful how the staff were suddenly pulling together and how! I put it down to the fact that they were given the responsibility not only for thinking through the ideas but then being able to find out if everything had worked. Not only were the staff individually and collectively involved but I was able to monitor their reactions and gauge the success of the changes through the staff.'

When it comes to inspection, the work that the head and the setting staff have put into monitoring and evaluation often pays off. Patti emphasizes, 'Having gone so carefully through all our plans, it was a relatively simple matter to fill in the self-evaluation forms for OfSTED and to add many more examples to show that we had been doing and how much further we have to go. We also had to comply with local requirements, too, as we'd had money from a range of sources who all wanted to know how it had been spent to improve the quality and status of the setting and the care and education of the children.' The effective head understands clearly all the inspection requirements and compliance issues including a clear understanding of OfSTED frameworks and documents such as *Every Child Matters* (2.8d).

Stem 2.8	**Leaves 2.8a–2.8d**

An effective early years leader or manager should...

2.8 *Ensure effective implementation and monitoring of ideas*	2.8a *Ensure that plans are implemented efficiently and effectively (this involves sharing ideas with staff and parents whenever possible and, once an idea has become a plan or policy, committing to it completely)*
	2.8b *Ensure that deviations from plans are well conceived and decisions are made explicit (this involves monitoring and evaluating the implementation of ideas and being able to improvise them whilst involving others)*
	2.8c *Monitor all actions to ensure that the planning and implementation of ideas are analysed and evaluated (this may involve setting up a system for monitoring implementation and gauging its success)*
	2.8d *Understand inspection requirements and compliance issues (this involves having knowledge and understanding of OfSTED frameworks, Every Child Matters and other legal requirements)*
List your targets	
Formulate an action plan	

Reflect on your capabilities and complete the boxes ...

What are your strengths?
Which areas need improvement?
What can you do to build on your strengths?
What do you need to do to improve your skills and
capabilities?

What are your strengths?
Which areas need improvement?
What can you do to build on your strengths?
What do you need to do to improve your skills and
capabilities?

What are your strengths?
Which areas need improvement?
What can you do to build on your strengths?
What do you need to do to improve your skills and
capabilities?

What are your strengths?
Which areas need improvement?
What can you do to build on your strengths?
What do you need to do to improve your skills and
capabilities?

Use this space for writing

Stem 2.9	**Leaves 2.9a–2.9c**

An effective early years leader or manager should . . .

2.9 Ensure effective operation of basic administrative procedures	*2.9a Understand procedures for the admission and registration of children (this involves devising settling-in programmes for all children, as well as having systems in place for monitoring admission and retention)*

	2.9b Understand the need for and the implementation of appropriate records of children and staff (this involves having good organizational skills and having the ability to discern appropriate information for recording)

	2.9c Understand how to budget effectively and appreciate the importance of securing funding, financial planning and transparent accounting (this involves having knowledge of useable models for budgeting)

List your targets	
Formulate an action plan	

Reflect on your capabilities and complete the boxes...

What are your strengths?
Which areas need improvement?
What can you do to build on your strengths?
What do you need to do to improve your skills and capabilities?

What are your strengths?
Which areas need improvement?
What can you do to build on your strengths?
What do you need to do to improve your skills and capabilities?

What are your strengths?
Which areas need improvement?
What can you do to build on your strengths?
What do you need to do to improve your skills and capabilities?

Use this space for writing

Use this space for writing

Stem 2.10	**Leaves 2.10a–2.10e**

An effective early years leader or manager should . . .

2.10 Ensure effective physical resource management and administration (continued on next page)	*2.10a Ensure acquisition and effective utilization of resources (this involves making sure that adequate resources are available and then making sure that they are used effectively and economically, realizing the need for monitoring systems)*
	2.10b Have knowledge of strategies for systematic resourcing and implement them (this involves having both financial and educational experience, and being able to match resources to the curriculum and child development)
	2.10c Ensure effective financial management (this involves having an aptitude for finance, knowing all areas of the setting to ensure successful budgeting and allocation, and making successful bids for funding)
	2.10d Use the budget appropriately to provide optimally for children, staff and parents (this involves ensuring that children have the best possible resources without granting them automatic priority at others' expense)
	2.10e Take responsibility for the physical environment (this involves making sure that it is comfortable, safe, non-oppressive, multiculturally positive, stimulating, well-resourced and well-numbered)

List your targets	
Formulate an action plan	

Reflect on your capabilities and complete the boxes . . .

What are your strengths?
Which areas need improvement?
What can you do to build on your strengths?
What do you need to do to improve your skills and
capabilities?

What are your strengths?
Which areas need improvement?
What can you do to build on your strengths?
What do you need to do to improve your skills and
capabilities?

What are your strengths?
Which areas need improvement?
What can you do to build on your strengths?
What do you need to do to improve your skills and
capabilities?

What are your strengths?
Which areas need improvement?
What can you do to build on your strengths?
What do you need to do to improve your skills and
capabilities?

What are your strengths?
Which areas need improvement?
What can you do to build on your strengths?
What do you need to do to improve your skills and
capabilities?

Stem 2.10 (cont.)	**Leaves 2.10f–2.10g**

An effective early years leader or manager should . . .

2.10 Ensure effective physical resource management and administration (continued from previous page)	*2.10f Have a special interest in the learning and teaching environment and ensure consensus amongst all involved (this involves ensuring that it is both stimulating and safe, optimizing physical and mental development with linguistic and sensorimotor stimuli)* 

	2.10g Ensure a safe and healthy learning and working environment (this involves being familiar with the Children Act 2004, the Health and Safety at Work Act 1974, the Food Safety Regulations Act 1995, and other relevant Acts) 

List your targets	
Formulate an action plan	

Reflect on your capabilities and complete the boxes . . .

What are your strengths?
Which areas need improvement?
What can you do to build on your strengths?
What do you need to do to improve your skills and
capabilities?

What are your strengths?
Which areas need improvement?
What can you do to build on your strengths?
What do you need to do to improve your skills and
capabilities?

Use this space for writing

Use this space for writing

Use this space for writing

5 The Professional Skills and Attributes branch

Introduction

Regardless of the profession, there are certain professional skills and attributes that all leaders and heads require. Heads of early years settings are no exception. The skills and attributes contained in this section are, therefore, mainly those which can be classed as 'universal' or 'generic' professional skills.

In recent years, more professional, and formalized, approaches to 'educare' in the early years have meant significant changes in the ways settings are managed, with the consequent need for heads to demonstrate not only high level commercial skills but also exceptional professional skills and attributes. It is these on which we focus in this section.

What does it mean to be 'professional'? Being professional depends, of course, on the profession. However, the term 'professional' is usually used to describe a person who is characterized by or conforms to the technical or ethical standards of a given profession; someone who is courteous, conscientious and 'businesslike' in the workplace, and well-informed and abreast of work-related ideas and developments. Some people see a profession in contrast to the word 'occupation', which refers generally to the nature of a person's employment rather than to the ways in which they undertake that employment. Each group of professionals tends to have its own code of practice (or ethics) in relation to its work which is understood and adhered to by all those within that profession. The code of practice can, as in the case of early years heads, be mainly unwritten yet still guide the professionals involved in their day-to-day practices.

With the rise of this greater professionalism in the early years, employing suitably qualified staff (3.1) and ensuring a strong policy of continual professional development training and reflection are crucial. All staff should be considered to be professional, including the head. It could be argued that with this rise in professionalism and the demand for consistently high quality provision, the role of early years head has become both more complex and more professional in recent years. In a complex job and in a complex environment, problems are bound to arise: the need for effective problem solving (3.2) becomes paramount.

Another result of early years management becoming more complex and demanding is the need for efficient time management (3.3). A head has many different tasks to undertake and many people to whom they are accountable and for whom they are responsible. Organizational efficiency – making the most of the time available – is crucial. One of the most important ways of ensuring good use of time and a well-organized and efficient setting is good communication (3.4).

The demand for increased professionalism has also affected the number of people involved in the provision of the service. Consequently, an effective early years head needs to have good diplomatic and conflict resolution skills (3.5). Heads have the unenviable task of trying to keep everyone informed and happy. This demands many essential high-level skills such as:

- being diplomatic;
- being an active listener;

- having the ability to diffuse an argument and use compromise effectively;
- handling and disseminating paperwork of various kinds;
- being a mediator, sounding-board and negotiator;
- being able to mediate in potentially heated discussions;
- ensuring honesty as well as professional courtesy and respect between those involved.

The skills and attributes outlined briefly in this introduction are overarching, representing broad areas of a head's professional skills, within which many other varied and detailed skills and attributes are included. These skills also relate to the fourth, and final, branch of ELMS: Personal Characteristics and Attitudes.

Stem 3.1	**Leaves 3.1a–3.1d**

An effective early years leader or manager should...

3.1 Promote the formalization of staff qualifications	*3.1a Have a high level of formal accreditation relevant to early years management (this may involve having qualifications from the two separate fields of business management and childcare, nursery nursing or teaching)*
	3.1b Promote and support staff to achieve a high level of accreditation relevant to the early years profession (this involves encouraging staff to engage and practice educational theory, as well as study for awards)
	3.1c Ensure that self and staff have the opportunity for ongoing and relevant professional development (this involves ensuring that staff are aware of opportunities, receive financial backing and receive time remission)
	3.1d Ensure that adequate resources, time and money are invested in staff and their training (this involves having a training budget and ensuring that resources are suited to school aims and staff attributes)

List your targets	
Formulate an action plan	

eflect on your capabilities and complete the boxes ...

What are your strengths?
Which areas need improvement?
What can you do to build on your strengths?
What do you need to do to improve your skills and
capabilities?

What are your strengths?
Which areas need improvement?
What can you do to build on your strengths?
What do you need to do to improve your skills and
capabilities?

What are your strengths?
Which areas need improvement?
What can you do to build on your strengths?
What do you need to do to improve your skills and
capabilities?

What are your strengths?
Which areas need improvement?
What can you do to build on your strengths?
What do you need to do to improve your skills and
capabilities?

Use this space for writing

Stem 3.2	**Leaves 3.2a–3.2c**

An effective early years leader or manager should . . .

3.2 Be an effective problem solver	3.2a Be able to recognize, identify and diagnose problems (these may be professional or relational, educational or emotional, or connected to communication or confidence, to name just a few possibilities)

	3.2b Be able to solve problems and facilitate problem solving amongst others (this involves having the capacity to think laterally about problems and provide support for staff, demanding energy, pragmatism and resourcefulness)

	3.2c Be reflective about own leadership and managerial role to ensure that the process of self-improvement is continuous and enhances performance (this involves being self-aware and reflective, whilst at the same time being self-assured and confident)

List your targets	
Formulate an action plan	

eflect on your capabilities and complete the boxes . . .

What are your strengths?
Which areas need improvement?
What can you do to build on your strengths?
What do you need to do to improve your skills and
capabilities?

What are your strengths?
Which areas need improvement?
What can you do to build on your strengths?
What do you need to do to improve your skills and
capabilities?

What are your strengths?
Which areas need improvement?
What can you do to build on your strengths?
What do you need to do to improve your skills and
capabilities?

Use this space for writing

Use this space for writing

Stem 3.3 Have effective time management skills

Cameo: Maxine

'The main barrier to getting things done is interruption; ... by handling interruptions, coping with them and minimizing them, everything suddenly becomes easier.' This is the advice of Maxine, the head of a large town-based playschool. 'Interruptions and prioritization, these are two things that are very important to my time management. The former I avoid wherever possible, the latter I do whenever possible.' An effective early years head should therefore have the ability to prioritize actions for oneself and others (3.3a).

Telephone calls, not to mention e-mails, can be a major barrier to getting things done. Unfortunately, the telephone and the computer are the main links to the outside world, and for this reason have a profound significance in early years provision. Today we live in a culture of 'blame', where parents are suspicious of other adults, and so the need to be open and accessible is of paramount importance. 'The phone is a constant distraction, and does make my time management more difficult,' says Maxine. 'But as a rule I try to keep phone conversations short and to the point. This is one way I've learnt to deal with external interruptions.' An effective early years head should find ways to ensure time is used effectively and disruptions are kept to a minimum (3.3b).

'There are plenty of time-saving devices in the shops these days, at very affordable prices,' Maxine continues. 'I have an answering machine in my office that enables me temporarily to ignore calls, most of which are not immediately important or urgent. When you're calling someone back you have more control over the conversation. Indeed, the caller determines when the call comes to an end. We also have other devices ... computers, a photocopier and a fax machine.'

Maxine believes that good time management consists of two things: efficiency and effectiveness. 'Good time management is not necessarily about being busy. Being busy means that you are filling time, not that you are utilizing it well. I went on a time management course once and I learnt there that it's not just about doing something well (efficiency), it's about doing the right thing well (effectiveness). This comes from the head but must be echoed by staff. All my staff are, in the main, both efficient and effective professionals.'

One of the most important manifestations of efficiency and effectiveness is punctuality, which includes meeting deadlines. In the same way that a herd moves only as fast as its slowest runner, weak professional practice can be extremely detrimental to the setting. Effective early years heads should therefore encourage punctuality and deadline meeting in staff (3.3c).

Another essential skill in time management is handling 'bureaucracy'. Today's workplace is flooded with paperwork, as the need for accountability and transparency mounts. Management is no longer about being 'the best' practitioner: it is about being the most organized and energetic, and the most competent administrator: the best juggler. This is where heads most often come unstuck. Effective early years heads should therefore ensure effective handling of paperwork (3.3d).

Table 5.1 is a modified version of a 'task efficiency audit' recommended by Lyus (1998: 128) to assess the effectiveness of an individual's time management. Some readers may find it helpful as an *aide-memoire*.

Table 5.1   Task efficiency audit

Efficiency technique	Use of time
1 Style	Make sure your working *style* suits your temperament
2 Proforma	Whenever possible, have standardized and common ways of doing things – *proforma*
3 Interlink	Whenever possible, *link* things together and consolidate – kill two birds with one stone
4 Redistribute	Whenever possible, delegate tasks and distribute the work amongst staff – *redistribute* as relevant
5 Anticipate	Whenever possible, make preparations for and *anticipate* likely occurrences – use your instincts!
6 Legitimize	Make sure the means is suited to the end and that there is not an easier way of doing it – *legitimize*!

Source: Based on Lyus (1998: 128)

Stem 3.3	Leaves 3.3a–3.3d

An effective early years leader or manager should . . .

3.3 Have effective time management skills	*3.3a Have the ability to prioritize actions for self and others (this involves ensuring effective and efficient use of time, utilizing rather than 'filling' what time you do have, and being able to delegate as well as focus)*

	3.3b Ensure time is used effectively and disruptions kept to a minimum (this involves developing time-saving strategies and investing in time-saving devices, as well as allocating and communicating)

	3.3c Promote punctuality and ensure staff meet deadlines (this involves leading by example and ensuring goals, objectives and deadlines are explicit and realistic, and interdependence amongst staff encouraged)

	3.3d Ensure effective handling and dissemination of paperwork (this involves bureaucratic competence and excellent organizational skills, which may be developed through administrative or secretarial training courses)

List your targets	
Formulate an action plan	

Reflect on your capabilities and complete the boxes ...

What are your strengths?
Which areas need improvement?
What can you do to build on your strengths?
What do you need to do to improve your skills and
capabilities?

What are your strengths?
Which areas need improvement?
What can you do to build on your strengths?
What do you need to do to improve your skills and
capabilities?

What are your strengths?
Which areas need improvement?
What can you do to build on your strengths?
What do you need to do to improve your skills and
capabilities?

What are your strengths?
Which areas need improvement?
What can you do to build on your strengths?
What do you need to do to improve your skills and
capabilities?

Use this space for writing

Stem 3.4 Have good communication and discourse skills

Cameo: Ali

'The importance of communication in early years provision is generally underestimated,' says Ali, a long-term head of a successful private nursery. 'A good early years head communicates differently with 3-year-olds from how she does with 4- or 5-year-olds. Besides this, communicating with staff, some of whom will be older and more experienced than others, requires a completely different approach; not to mention the approach with parents and other important adults.'

An effective early years head should encourage good and appropriate communication between management and staff (3.4a) and encourage good and appropriate communication between staff and children (3.4b). Effective communication limits the amount of misunderstanding and neglect, enabling the smooth running of the service.

Ali has been an early years head for over ten years; she was a nursery nurse for ten years before that. She has therefore witnessed numerous changes in the early years profession. 'One of the most significant changes has been the increased emphasis on communication and dialogue.' Because of the nature of the service, early years heads should have excellent verbal communication skills (3.4c).

Because Ali has been a nursery nurse, she has a heightened awareness of the importance of good communication from management to staff. 'I remember when I first started nursery nursing: the first head I had would often keep us in the dark, she rarely handed out praise, and she didn't make herself approachable. None of us knew whether we were doing a good job or not. There was no real dialogue going on, which created a barrier between staff and management ... in fact, between members of staff too. The head should be the culture setter, and because of this particular head's attitude, the nursery was not conducive to communication. She must have had years of experience ... and she kept it from us.'

'When my husband and I moved, I got a job in the local nursery, and the culture of the place couldn't have been more different. The head communicated with us, she listened sensitively, and she was adamant that communication should be a two-way process. Her communication skills had a ripple effect. I learnt from these experiences that good communication is the foundation on which to build a really empowering, satisfying and democratic workplace. I always encourage friendly and sensitive communication amongst my staff' (3.4d).

In early years provision, the likelihood of communication breakdown is high because of the potential for interruption, noise and competition for attention. 'Interruption is the main barrier to good communication,' says Ali, 'so something I make a point of doing is limiting the chance of this happening when I am communicating something important. We have weekly meetings and my office is usually fairly quiet ... a good alternative to the noisy backdrop of the nursery rooms.'

A common misconception is that messages are registered and understood in the same way regardless of who receives them. There are, however, psychological barriers to understanding, so for every different person who receives a message there is the potential for a different interpretation and understanding. Because the early years profession is dominated by subjective beliefs, values and viewpoints, these psychological barriers may be more problematical and have more impact than in other professions where there is more of a consensus opinion. Every practitioner has a philosophy and a view of 'how things should be done'. Whilst this is obviously positive, a good early years head should account for this and be particularly conscious of their delivery of the message, also ensuring that it is as unambiguous as possible. An effective early years head, therefore, should encourage accurate understanding through discussion and explanation (3.4e).

Ali has been to a couple of communications workshops. 'One of them concentrated on listening, being an "active listener", which means really trying hard to listen to someone without the distraction of building up your own argument and thinking about the next thing you want to say – something most of us do all the time. People "pretend" to listen to the person who is talking but really concentrate on their own agenda.' An effective early years head should be an active listener who focuses on what the person is both saying and meaning (3.4f).

'The other workshop was about our individual ways of communicating. One thing I noticed about myself is that I often used the pronoun "you" when addressing staff, especially when I was addressing an issue or making a criticism. This immediately pointed the finger and put my members of staff on the defensive. Now I use "I" when addressing a problem. This distances the problem from the member of staff and tends to get a much better response.' In as many ways as possible, the effective early years head should reflect on one's own style of communication and encourage non-oppressive communication between staff and management which is sensitive and honest (3.4g).

'It is also easy to forget the importance of parents,' Ali says. 'Some heads see parents as peripheral, even as interfering with nursery practices, forgetting that good communications between parents and staff can make everyone's lives easier, and forgetting that the child is a huge part of the parents' lives. Other heads, such as my first one, go to the other extreme, pandering to the parents and in the process neglecting the children and their staff. A balance must be achieved.' An effective early years head, therefore, should encourage sensitive, responsive and friendly communication with parents (3.4h).

As Ali says, being able to communicate with different individuals is also very important. 'I am in constant contact with the local authority, the local media, government officials . . . the list goes on.' Effective early years heads must have beneficial open communication with the wider community (3.4i).

In short, the currency of communication is information. Good communication means that all the most important and relevant information is going to the right people delivered in a way that makes it appropriate for everyone. Perhaps most importantly of all, an effective early years head should ensure that children, staff, management, parents and the wider community are well-informed and involved (3.4j).

Stem 3.4	Leaves 3.4a–3.4e

An effective early years leader or manager should . . .

3.4 Have good communication and discourse skills (continued on next page)	3.4a Promote high quality and effective communication between management and staff (this involves ensuring that channels of communication are built on professional honesty, respect, personal courtesy, fun and friendship)
	3.4b Promote high quality and effective communication between staff and children (this involves ensuring that staff are able to engage and control children, and able to tailor their communication to suit the receiver)
	3.4c Have excellent oral and written communication skills (this involves being articulate and engaging, being able to overcome psychological barriers to good communication and determine what is worth disseminating to staff)
	3.4d Promote friendly and sensitive communication and networking (this involves being attentive, receptive and responsive to staff and parents whilst encouraging them to do likewise to one another)
	3.4e Promote accurate understanding through discussion and explanation (this involves ensuring that time is allotted and an arena provided for the satisfactory exploration of important issues)

List your targets	
Formulate an action plan	

Reflect on your capabilities and complete the boxes . . .

What are your strengths?
Which areas need improvement?
What can you do to build on your strengths?
What do you need to do to improve your skills and
capabilities?

What are your strengths?
Which areas need improvement?
What can you do to build on your strengths?
What do you need to do to improve your skills and
capabilities?

What are your strengths?
Which areas need improvement?
What can you do to build on your strengths?
What do you need to do to improve your skills and
capabilities?

What are your strengths?
Which areas need improvement?
What can you do to build on your strengths?
What do you need to do to improve your skills and
capabilities?

What are your strengths?
Which areas need improvement?
What can you do to build on your strengths?
What do you need to do to improve your skills and
capabilities?

Stem 3.4 (cont.)	Leaves 3.4f–3.4j

An effective early years leader or manager should . . .

3.4 Have good communication and discourse skills (continued from previous page)	3.4f Be an active listener and a sensitive, empathic responder (this involves listening to whoever is speaking without thinking about your reply or whether you agree, without prejudice, preconception or interruption, and encouraging others to do the same)
	3.4g Promote honest but sensitive communication between staff and management (this involves being willing to defer to other members of staff when necessary, being an 'open' leader rather than a 'closed' authoritarian)
	3.4h Promote responsive, sensitive and friendly communication with parents (this involves creating an approach from staff where children are seen in their family context and parents are seen as partners from whom staff can learn)
	3.4i Ensure mutually beneficial communication with the wider community (this involves cultivating channels of communication with relevant sources, such as regional groups, publishers, health authorities and other professionals)
	3.4j Ensure that children, staff, parents and the wider community are well-informed and involved (this involves ensuring that the right information is going to the right people, at the right time, in the right way)

List your targets	
Formulate an action plan	

Reflect on your capabilities and complete the boxes...

What are your strengths?
Which areas need improvement?
What can you do to build on your strengths?
What do you need to do to improve your skills and
capabilities?

What are your strengths?
Which areas need improvement?
What can you do to build on your strengths?
What do you need to do to improve your skills and
capabilities?

What are your strengths?
Which areas need improvement?
What can you do to build on your strengths?
What do you need to do to improve your skills and
capabilities?

What are your strengths?
Which areas need improvement?
What can you do to build on your strengths?
What do you need to do to improve your skills and
capabilities?

What are your strengths?
Which areas need improvement?
What can you do to build on your strengths?
What do you need to do to improve your skills and
capabilities?

Stem 3.5 Have excellent diplomacy and conflict resolution skills

Cameo: Susan

Susan, the head of a private nursery, used to view conflict as a negative occurrence, avoiding it wherever possible. She often felt depressed when disagreements and tensions arose. Now she is philosophical about conflict. 'I have learnt that conflict is quite often a blessing in disguise.'

Susan now views conflict as a positive occurrence rather than abnormal. 'Where there is no conflict, there is no honesty.' She no longer sees instances of conflict as a reflection of poor management and leadership. 'It can cement group relationships,' she suggests, 'as well as enable personal and professional growth and development.' Often, conflict is the release of underlying tensions and unsatisfied needs. Susan approaches conflict resolution systematically, attempting to identify the original problem and to mediate solutions.

One innovation she undertook was to modify the structure of her nursery. 'Because of the nature of early years provision, and due to the fact that my nursery is open for twelve hours a day and children need constant supervision, most of my staff are on shift work, which means that there are few occasions available for formal staff meetings. The lack of contact time between me and the staff, and the staff with one another, meant that communication in the nursery was initially very poor. This generated a lot of conflict. The best counter-measure for this seemed to be to set aside a time each week for meeting with one another. These meetings operated like open forums, where problems could be addressed and information could be disseminated, and most importantly, I could be receptive to suggestions (3.5a). The weekly meeting has now come to be quite a social event with staff bringing in "goodies" to share.'

In averting conflict, one important thing is to balance the existence of shared values and goals with the need to make the best of individual differences in terms of skill and personality. The profession is dominated by subjective beliefs, values and viewpoints (Moyles and Adams 2001), and these can be used effectively rather than suppressed. An effective early years head should be able to negotiate, respect, and utilize different viewpoints (3.5b). 'I have adopted a democratic rather than an authoritarian leadership style,' says Susan, 'because this seems to minimize conflict. The staff feel empowered and communication is two-way. I can act as a sounding-board for different people and that way conflict is often nipped in the bud' (3.5c).

'Another thing that generated a lot of conflict was job expectations and role definitions. When I first started managing the nursery, I did not clearly define the roles and responsibilities of my staff. This caused many problems because even I was confused as to exactly who was responsible for doing what. I was often unsure as to whether I was asking things beyond the call of duty or even beyond individual capabilities. I then changed things drastically by writing up a list of job descriptions. Moreover, I resolved that a prescribed way of doing things was the only way to increase effectiveness and standardize practices. The problem with this approach was that most of my staff felt demotivated by having their own ideas rejected. A few members of staff said that they felt that their creativity and initiative had been taken away. I needed to find the middle ground, and I achieved this by loosely defining everyone's role and status. The result was that the staff felt as though they had direction and set responsibilities, but also room to manoeuvre, without me breathing down their necks.'

As Susan pointed out when describing her open forums, the dissemination of information is another important way of averting conflicts. Much information comes to early years settings through the head. This could be withheld and used to create a power divide between those who are 'in the know' and those who are not. Better professional practice would be to use information to empower and assist staff in making their own joint and more informed decisions.

Communication is perhaps the most important factor in averting and resolving conflict. All those in early years settings have needs and should be able to voice them. Susan's open forum is one way of ensuring that voices are heard and heads are able to listen actively to staff and act as a mediator as necessary (3.5c).

Another possible area of conflict relates to parents. In most early years settings, the drop-off and pick-up times are very short because both parents and staff have things to do. Conflict, and especially conflict of interest, may therefore arise between parents and staff. Susan has a way of countering this problem. 'I try to encourage parents to hang around for a few minutes when dropping off and picking up their children to become acquainted with the members of staff who are responsible for their child and start profitable discussions. This is not always possible, of course, but extra effort when and where necessary can be made. This was another simple measure I took to resolve conflict. Often using this means, conflict was averted.' Susan was able to encourage staff to listen actively to parents (3.5d). Needless to say, she too listened to parents and was rewarded by hearing several say how useful it was to talk with staff at the beginning and end of the day.

As well as staff and parents, effective early years heads should also listen actively to the children (3.5e). Although opinion is still divided as to whether it is essential for an early years head to have had experience with children at the level of carer or teacher, it is not in doubt that the children's views and needs should receive appropriate attention. A good early years head must ensure that the interests of all groups involved are satisfied and met in accordance with their respective importance in the ultimate process.

Sometimes conflicts between individuals are impossible to avert, despite well-considered, preventative measures and structural modifications. Often this can be attributed to a 'personality clash' which brings an air of helplessness and defeatism. But just because two members of staff are not expressly compatible does not mean that they cannot come to a professional working consensus. Compromise, deference to the greater good, mutual respect and mutual understanding for the importance of different types of people, especially in early years settings, are what an effective early years head should encourage in members of staff. The head must be able to resolve tension between individuals in an impartial and diplomatic manner, understanding the need for compromise (3.5f).

As Susan concludes: 'An exemplary head should be capable of resolving and where possible averting conflict' (3.5g). Indeed, it is as important to be able to find ways of averting and minimizing conflict by making structural changes as it is to resolve them through diplomatic means. 'An effective head should understand internal conflicts and how they can best be resolved (3.5h). Internal conflicts, though, can more often than not be minimized through preventative measures.'

As Susan tells us, an effective early years head should take a calm and positive approach to conflicts and crises (3.5i). Conflict is not always negative but can lead to some interesting and exciting innovations.

One method of averting and resolving problems is to encourage your staff to be assertive and proactive, approaching the head immediately when they encounter a problem. Below is a useful 'assertiveness format' that a head may want to encourage the staff to use (Rodd 1998: 69). The assertiveness format proposes that the person in question should make four admissions about something creating conflict:

When . . .	(description of, for example, actions or issues)
I feel . . .	(description of feelings or emotions)
Because . . .	(explanation of importance or relevance)
I would prefer . . .	(indication of a decision or alternative)

An example here might be helpful written in the diary of a focus team member:

> When I want to communicate with a 'challenging' member of staff about her relationships with others, **I feel** uptight and expect resistance **because** she is known to respond very negatively to any seemingly critical comments from others. **I would prefer** that she and I sit down and talk around specific issues quietly over a cup of tea, so that I can let her explain to me the problem and how she thinks it might be resolved.

Stem 3.5	Leaves 3.5a–3.5e

An effective early years leader or manager should ...

3.5 Have excellent diplomacy and conflict resolution skills (continued on next page)	3.5a Be receptive to suggestions (this may involve setting aside some time each week to hold an open forum or another structured way of ensuring that staff have a voice and appreciate that their input is valued)
	3.5b Negotiate, respect and utilize different viewpoints (this involves enlisting staff expertise whenever possible, blending beliefs for complementary effect, and appreciating positive side-effects of contention)
	3.5c Listen actively to staff and undertake necessary mediation (this involves actively seeking out staff and affording them the opportunity to be frank and to exercise their opinions with the intention of instilling feelings of catharsis and ownership)
	3.5d Listen actively to parents and undertake necessary mediation (this involves actively seeking out parents during drop-off and pick-up times and starting constructive dialogues with the intention of instilling feelings of partnership and ownership)
	3.5e Listen actively to children (this involves searching beyond the articulated message to discern the unarticulated message of the child and in the process understanding children as abstract communicators)

List your targets	
Formulate an action plan	

Reflect on your capabilities and complete the boxes...

What are your strengths?
Which areas need improvement?
What can you do to build on your strengths?
What do you need to do to improve your skills and
capabilities?

What are your strengths?
Which areas need improvement?
What can you do to build on your strengths?
What do you need to do to improve your skills and
capabilities?

What are your strengths?
Which areas need improvement?
What can you do to build on your strengths?
What do you need to do to improve your skills and
capabilities?

What are your strengths?
Which areas need improvement?
What can you do to build on your strengths?
What do you need to do to improve your skills and
capabilities?

What are your strengths?
Which areas need improvement?
What can you do to build on your strengths?
What do you need to do to improve your skills and
capabilities?

Stem 3.5 (cont.)	Leaves 3.5f–3.5i

An effective early years leader or manager should . . .

3.5 Have excellent diplomacy and conflict resolution skills (continued from previous page)	3.5f Resolve tensions between individuals and understand compromise (this involves viewing conflict as a positive and natural occurrence, signalling that honesty and frustrations are not being suppressed, and being able to quell disagreement)
	3.5g Be capable of identifying, resolving and, where relevant, averting conflict (this may involve developing preventative measures and making structural modifications to minimize the possibility of unhealthy conflict)
	3.5h Understand internal conflicts and how they can be negotiated/resolved (this involves appreciating that conflict, in small measure, is more a sign that the setting is running normally than is the absence of conflict)
	3.5i Take a calm, positive and tolerant approach to conflicts and crises (this involves viewing conflict as a catalyst for positive change and a safety valve for discontent, approaching it, therefore, philosophically)

List your targets	
Formulate an action plan	

Reflect on your capabilities and complete the boxes...

What are your strengths?
Which areas need improvement?
What can you do to build on your strengths?
What do you need to do to improve your skills and
capabilities?

What are your strengths?
Which areas need improvement?
What can you do to build on your strengths?
What do you need to do to improve your skills and
capabilities?

What are your strengths?
Which areas need improvement?
What can you do to build on your strengths?
What do you need to do to improve your skills and
capabilities?

What are your strengths?
Which areas need improvement?
What can you do to build on your strengths?
What do you need to do to improve your skills and
capabilities?

Use this space for writing

6 The Personal Characteristics and Attitudes branch

Introduction

The preceding three chapters have, for the most part, identified the essential qualities, skills and attributes required of an effective early years head. This chapter focuses on other important factors: the personal characteristics and attitudes of the leader/manager. This is the branch on which to focus if you are evaluating the personal dimension of your role as an early years head. If ELMS is to be used as guidance in the recruitment of effective middle or senior managers/leaders for a setting, this section will be essential.

'Personal characteristics and attitudes' constitute all the many important traits, dispositions and interests that heads will possess to carry out their important and complex role. These are often difficult aspects to evaluate because a concept such as 'enthusiasm' has many different guises and, like many other process components, defies being 'behaviourized'. This is also particularly true of people's attitudes to their roles – how you feel about the role and your own ways of dealing with it will affect one's attitudes towards it. Most personal characteristics and attitudes are subjective and difficult to pin down in words or actions. By having these various characteristics and attitudes identified and documented, heads and other evaluators will be able not only to consider the wide range of characteristics that individual heads need to possess but also to undertake a process of identifying strengths and challenges.

A truly effective head will have significant professional and personal strengths, for example, enthusiasm for, and implicit and learned knowledge about, early years education and care (Ebbeck and Waninganayake 2002) (4.1). As a consequence of that enthusiasm and interest, effective heads will have relevant knowledge and, in particular, will understand the principles and theories underpinning their professional role. Anyone who is really interested in something will usually read about it and become receptive to all new knowledge offered.

Effective heads tend to have strong principles and specific (if sometimes unarticulated) values. They want to provide a quality service because of their belief in children and the rights of children and parents, and because they appreciate their responsibilities to the setting, the community and to society in general. Central to this are the transitions that children make from setting to setting and from pre-school to school (4.2); heads and their staff should be able to make these as smooth as possible and provide a firm foundation on which other settings and schools can build (Fabian and Dunlop 2002). Similarly, all aspects of children's development and learning (4.4) are of overriding interest and concern for committed early years heads.

Indeed, heads will often be attracted to the profession for intrinsic reasons (4.3). Childcare is often underpaid in relation to the level of knowledge, skills and understanding required: working hours are often long, even anti-social in those settings that provide long-term care and education. This is the nature of this job, so as well as their own acceptance of the parameters of the role, heads need also to encourage staff to enjoy the job for its intrinsic value – and often significant personal and professional reward (Fullan 2003). Much of this reward comes from having daily close contact with young children and the sense of undertaking a worthwhile role in ensuring they develop to their fullest potential during the time they spend in the setting. This entails having a continued commitment to, and vested interest in, children's overall development and learning (4.4).

Ambition is central to the professional and personal dimensions of the head's role and for the continued advancement of the setting (4.5). First and foremost, ambition should stem from the head in the form of a strong desire for improvement as one of the key defining characteristics (Yorke-Barr 2001).

An early years setting is a creative environment; things are constantly being invented, imagined, explored, modelled, drawn, painted and evolved (Duffy 2004). A head needs to have an approach advocating creative intelligence (4.6), affording both children and staff the opportunity to express themselves and their ideas freely and to feel valued. The early years setting is an environment full of different emotions – indeed, dealing with young children means that early years professionals draw on their emotions to facilitate the daily undertaking of their job (Moyles 2001). Early years educators frequently use words such as 'passionate' to describe themselves and their attitudes to working and playing with young children. Steinberg and Kincheloe's (1998) research into students' responses to analysing their experiences explain: 'Little ... learning takes place until ... our passions are engaged ... [and] intellect, academic knowledge and personal experience are brought together'. A head should have an approach advocating the sensitive development of emotional intelligence within and across the setting (4.7). As Sharp (2002) indicates, emotional intelligence is the main aptitude considered to account for outstanding performance in top leaders.

Heads deal with a plethora of different people involved in childcare and education. Some are responsible for well over a hundred people, both adults and children. As was highlighted in the Introduction, being the head of an early years setting has become increasingly a role as leader/manager of a small business enterprise. There are hundreds of issues and concerns, from staff feelings to legal decisions, such as those associated with special needs. An effective head will have an infectious (self-)awareness (4.8) and the ability to handle a wealth of diverse events, practices and decisions (Riley and MacBeath 2003) in a sensitive, empathic and caring manner whilst ensuring that decisions meet the needs of all across the setting.

Undertaking anything that is challenging is made easier if one has a good sense of humour. Clearly, this means laughing with (not at) children and adults. Play and seeing the funny side of life have more significance in early years settings than in the majority of other small businesses, so an effective early years head should have a strong affinity to play and understand the importance of fun and play (4.9).

Stem 4.1 Have knowledge of, and a natural enthusiasm for, children, teaching and learning

Cameo: Amrit

'Some nurseries have a strict policy of no contact ... never be alone with a child, don't sit them on your lap, don't cuddle them. ... In other words, don't express yourself physically. ... We don't subscribe to that here. Parents are told that we encourage affection and physical contact at the nursery. That's our ethic of caring, I suppose.'

Amrit is the head of a nursery. She has strong views about nursery nurses and believes that the service has the dual responsibility of teaching and caring for its children. 'Children need to be cuddled, reassured, comforted; ... they need you to help them change, to toilet train them. ... Refraining from physical contact is just not possible. In a way it isn't such an issue in nurseries. It's more an issue in primary schools where you tend to get more male teachers. We don't have any male nursery staff here. That's not to say I wouldn't welcome a male member of staff. But men, unfortunately for them, invite suspicion. You can take measures though: ... put a cushion on your lap when you sit children on it, just to make absolutely sure that your intentions cannot be misread.' Early years heads and their staff have a commitment to both the children and their education. An effective early years head should believe in and value the dual responsibility of early years providers to care and to teach (4.1a).

'The way I look at it', says Amrit, 'is that you can take a horse to water but you can't make it drink. You can talk to children, but you can't guarantee that they'll be listening to you, nor can you guarantee that what you've said has been understood. I think that relating to the child and gaining respect and trust are the only sure way of guaranteeing their attention and concentration. Being liked is essential for good learning. Young children have limited attention and interest, and so being approachable and able to package information in an interesting way is really important.'

Amrit supports the idea of a partnership between the nursery and the home. 'In the entrance we have a framed cross-stitch that says *In loco parentis*, which is Latin for "in place of the parent". It's kind of our motto. We believe that nursery staff are like surrogate parents. Because we're completely open about this approach, parents tend to be openly supportive and encouraging.' An effective early years head should understand the concept of *in loco parentis* (4.1b).

'Children have two sides to them as well, which can be expressed in terms of caring and teaching. One side is the vulnerable, dependent side, which can be developed through caring, whilst the other side is the independent, individual one, which can be developed through good teaching practices.' An effective early years head should understand children as reliant and vulnerable (4.1c) but at the same time understand children as independent and individual (4.1d).

'Children have a number of roles themselves,' Amrit continues. 'They are family members as well as playgroup members, extensions of their parents. They are also connected to the wider community. We are, as the saying goes, "working today for tomorrow".' An effective early years head is aware of this and conceptualizes children as individuals, family members and community members (4.1e, 4.1f, 4.1g). Young children are complex, capable and multifaceted – definitely not to be underestimated.

Stem 4.1	Leaves 4.1a–4.1e

An effective early years leader or manager should . . .

4.1 Have knowledge of, and a natural enthusiasm for, children, teaching and learning (continued on next page)	4.1a Understand and value the dual responsibility of early years providers to care, to ensure learning and to teach (this involves having a strong ethic of caring and believing in a partnership between the setting and the home)
	4.1b Understand the concept of 'in loco parentis' (this is a Latin phrase meaning 'in the place of the parent', used by educational specialists to describe the parental role played by early years professionals)
	4.1c Understand children as intelligent but vulnerable (this involves placing emphasis on the practitioner as carer above teacher where necessary, ensuring that all children are appropriately supported)
	4.1d Understand children as independent and individual (this involves placing emphasis on the practitioner as teacher above carer, where necessary, and ensuring that all children are appropriately supported)
	4.1e Conceptualize each child as unique (this involves ensuring that individual needs are met and provision is made for tailored curricula, offering one-on-one services such as settling-in programmes)

List your targets	
Formulate an action plan	

Reflect on your capabilities and complete the boxes...

What are your strengths?
Which areas need improvement?
What can you do to build on your strengths?
What do you need to do to improve your skills and
capabilities?

What are your strengths?
Which areas need improvement?
What can you do to build on your strengths?
What do you need to do to improve your skills and
capabilities?

What are your strengths?
Which areas need improvement?
What can you do to build on your strengths?
What do you need to do to improve your skills and
capabilities?

What are your strengths?
Which areas need improvement?
What can you do to build on your strengths?
What do you need to do to improve your skills and
capabilities?

What are your strengths?
Which areas need improvement?
What can you do to build on your strengths?
What do you need to do to improve your skills and
capabilities?

Stem 4.1 (cont.)	**Leaves 4.1f–4.1g**

An effective early years leader or manager should...

4.1 Have knowledge of, and a natural enthusiasm for, children, teaching and learning (continued from previous page)	4.1f Conceptualize children as family members (this involves ensuring good communication with parents and understanding children as extensions of self on the part of the parents, seeing them within their family context)

	4.1g Conceptualize children as community members (this involves ensuring that all staff fulfil their responsibility of cultivating good morals, ethics and etiquette in the adults of the future, of setting them an example)

List your targets	
Formulate an action plan	

eflect on your capabilities and complete the boxes...

| What are your strengths? |
| Which areas need improvement? |
| What can you do to build on your strengths? |
| What do you need to do to improve your skills and capabilities? |

What are your strengths?
Which areas need improvement?
What can you do to build on your strengths?
What do you need to do to improve your skills and capabilities?

Use this space for writing

Use this space for writing

Use this space for writing

Stem 4.2	Leaves 4.2a–4.2d

An effective early years leader or manager should...

4.2 Have a strong commitment to the settings-to-school transitions of the child	*4.2a Ensure the essential social progress of the child (this involves striving to ensure that the child is behaviourally and morally sound, confident and articulate, polite, and has a high self-concept)*
	4.2b Ensure the essential academic progress of the child (this involves ensuring that the child is at the appropriate level in relation to the Foundation Stage, with well-developed literacy and linguistic skill)
	4.2c Have strong background experience and understanding of children (this involves having some pre-setting involvement with children, either theoretically or practically, to ensure a high level of ability and suitability with the profession)
	4.2d Cultivate good relations and communications with the schools to which the children will transfer (this involves arranging mutual visits, transferring records and organizing settling-in programmes)

List your targets	
Formulate an action plan	

Reflect on your capabilities and complete the boxes...

What are your strengths?
Which areas need improvement?
What can you do to build on your strengths?
What do you need to do to improve your skills and
capabilities?

What are your strengths?
Which areas need improvement?
What can you do to build on your strengths?
What do you need to do to improve your skills and
capabilities?

What are your strengths?
Which areas need improvement?
What can you do to build on your strengths?
What do you need to do to improve your skills and
capabilities?

What are your strengths?
Which areas need improvement?
What can you do to build on your strengths?
What do you need to do to improve your skills and
capabilities?

Use this space for writing

Stem 4.3	Leaves 4.3a–4.3c

An effective early years leader or manager should . . .

4.3 Have an attraction to the profession for intrinsic rather than extrinsic reasons	4.3a Be interested in and fulfil the important components of the job as specific to early years (this involves having a natural interest in the early years as a subject and empathy for children in general)

	4.3b Fulfil with interest and commitment the important components of the job in relation to leadership, management and administration (this involves having a natural interest and disposition towards leadership and management)

	4.3c Understand the universal components of the role of head of setting (this involves being fully aware of the demands and rigours of being an early years manager and having realistic expectations of setting, self and others)

List your targets	
Formulate an action plan	

Reflect on your capabilities and complete the boxes ...

What are your strengths?
Which areas need improvement?
What can you do to build on your strengths?
What do you need to do to improve your skills and
capabilities?

What are your strengths?
Which areas need improvement?
What can you do to build on your strengths?
What do you need to do to improve your skills and
capabilities?

What are your strengths?
Which areas need improvement?
What can you do to build on your strengths?
What do you need to do to improve your skills and
capabilities?

Use this space for writing

Use this space for writing

Stem 4.4	Leaves 4.4a–4.4d

An effective early years leader or manager should...

4.4 Have a continued commitment to and vested interest in children's overall development	4.4a Understand the intellectual/cognitive development of children (this involves understanding key early years theories and theorists who inform early childhood care and education)
	4.4b Understand the physical development of children, including both fine-motor and gross-motor skills (this may involve having a working knowledge of relevant theories and subjects such as biology and physiology)
	4.4c Understand the social and cultural development of children (this may involve being able to recognize specific behaviours as signs of accelerated or delayed social development and being sensitive to communications)
	4.4d Understand the emotional and spiritual development of children (this may involve being able to recognize specific behaviours as indicative of the emotional state of a child, especially presented through play)

List your targets	
Formulate an action plan	

Reflect on your capabilities and complete the boxes ...

What are your strengths?
Which areas need improvement?
What can you do to build on your strengths?
What do you need to do to improve your skills and
capabilities?

What are your strengths?
Which areas need improvement?
What can you do to build on your strengths?
What do you need to do to improve your skills and
capabilities?

What are your strengths?
Which areas need improvement?
What can you do to build on your strengths?
What do you need to do to improve your skills and
capabilities?

What are your strengths?
Which areas need improvement?
What can you do to build on your strengths?
What do you need to do to improve your skills and
capabilities?

Use this space for writing

Stem 4.5	**Leaves 4.5a–4.5e**

An effective early years leader or manager should . . .

4.5 Have a strong sense of ambition and a strong desire for improvement (continued on next page)	*4.5a Have a commitment to long-term self-improvement (this involves being reflective and a 'life-long learner' but not at the expense of confidence and self-assurance, encouraging others to be similar)*

	4.5b Have a desire to improve the social/communicative self (this involves having the desire to support others' development and may involve organizing team-building activities, social events, forums and informal meetings)

	4.5c Have a desire to improve the professional self (this involves having the desire to support others' development as well as self, and may involve organizing training days, research activities and day trips)

	4.5d Have a desire to improve the setting and have realistic and appropriate ambitions for it (this involves ensuring that improvement goals are achievable and align with the values and abilities of the staff involved)

	4.5e Have an infectious and dynamic sense of ambition (this refers to having an inner drive to achieve and improve, of never being content or satisfied with self and setting, rather than fostering unrealistic and damaging aspirations)

List your targets	
Formulate an action plan	

Reflect on your capabilities and complete the boxes...

What are your strengths?
Which areas need improvement?
What can you do to build on your strengths?
What do you need to do to improve your skills and
capabilities?

What are your strengths?
Which areas need improvement?
What can you do to build on your strengths?
What do you need to do to improve your skills and
capabilities?

What are your strengths?
Which areas need improvement?
What can you do to build on your strengths?
What do you need to do to improve your skills and
capabilities?

What are your strengths?
Which areas need improvement?
What can you do to build on your strengths?
What do you need to do to improve your skills and
capabilities?

What are your strengths?
Which areas need improvement?
What can you do to build on your strengths?
What do you need to do to improve your skills and
capabilities?

Stem 4.5 (cont.)	Leaves 4.5f–4.5g

An effective early years leader or manager should . . .

4.5 Have a strong sense of ambition and a strong desire for improvement (continued from previous page)	4.5f Relay and instil ambition in the staff (this involves being able to inspire people and being the type of leader whom followers want to imitate in so far as they continually strive to extend boundaries and standards)	
	4.5g Relay and instil ambition in the children (this involves ensuring that staff cultivate high levels of self-value and morale in the children, who are given every opportunity to fulfil potential and develop aptitude)	

List your targets	
Formulate an action plan	

Reflect on your capabilities and complete the boxes...

What are your strengths?
Which areas need improvement?
What can you do to build on your strengths?
What do you need to do to improve your skills and
capabilities?

What are your strengths?
Which areas need improvement?
What can you do to build on your strengths?
What do you need to do to improve your skills and
capabilities?

Use this space for writing

Use this space for writing

Use this space for writing

Stem 4.6 Have an approach that advocates creative intelligence

Cameo: Daniela

'Creativity? It's a slippery concept! I can't really give a good definition of it, but I do try to encourage creativity, in my staff as well as in the children. I guess it's about imagination, exploration, and invention ... and originality.'

Daniela paints in watercolour in her spare time. She is someone whom other people often call artistic and creative. She is also the head of her village pre-school. 'Because I'm quite heavily into the arts myself, I try to encourage as much creativity in the playgroup as possible,' she says. Daniela's statement, whilst making positive claims about creativity and its place in early years provision, highlights some interesting associations and common misconceptions, namely that creativity is all about art.

Indeed, creativity and the arts are often used synonymously, as though they were interchangeable. This association implies that creativity does not exist outside of the arts. True to this school of thought, creative people are known as artistic geniuses, 'rare' and 'gifted' (Beetlestone 1999). The association invites a number of false divisions. Creative people are believed to be in the minority, with the rest comprising the majority. Furthermore, creativity is associated with play as opposed to work; work being an adult, serious and disciplined endeavour, whereas play is a childish, frivolous and undisciplined one.

In sum, over-associating creativity and art may have a damaging effect in a number of ways, especially in an early years context. Firstly, it may limit the opportunities that children have to express themselves creatively to just occasional pieces of art, such as drawings and paintings. Instead, creativity should be encouraged as a complete means of expression that can manifest itself in any context, including such disciplines as mathematics and science, as well as being an enjoyable and effective way of learning and teaching. Secondly, the overworked association between creativity and art may stop staff from approaching their work creatively because creativity can be characterized, by implication, as childish, frivolous and undisciplined.

However, in spite of her statement, Daniela does have a broad concept of what creativity is and how it can be used. 'With the government continually taking steps to formalize education, to make it all prescriptive, it is important to get children to exercise their creativity and to use their imagination and invention in everything they do. It is also a key process for learning effectively,' she continues. 'When you're presented with new information, in order to assimilate it and understand it you can't merely encounter it, you have to actually engage with it. It's the same for children. They won't learn anything as passive receivers, they have to be thoughtful and creative, and draw personal meaning from it.' An effective early years head will encourage the holistic development and expression of the creative capacity of all children (4.6a).

'The same is true for adults ... and therefore staff,' Daniela says, in reference to her previous statement about creativity enabling learning. 'My staff are encouraged to be creative in everything they do. It helps them to learn and it helps them to teach. Most importantly, it makes them more engaging and captivating to the children, so it helps the children learn too.' An effective early years head will encourage the holistic development and expression of the creative capacity of staff and encourage innovative and individual approaches by staff (Isles-Buck and Newstead 2003) (4.6b, 4.6c).

Although creativity does not refer expressly to art and does not therefore presuppose a physical product, creative outcomes are important for children, whether physical or not. 'When there is an end product, such as a drawing or a model, something that represents the creativity of the child, it is far easier to encourage them to be creative. It's hard to encourage and praise abstract thought because you can't see it. We do, therefore, give children as much opportunity as possible to make and build things . . . to express themselves . . . to be creative. We have that old proverb as our motto: "I hear and I forget; I see and I remember; I do and I understand".' As Daniela says, an effective early years head should understand children as inventors, builders and constructors (4.6d).

Communication skills come with increasing maturity. Children develop communication skills and rich vocabularies in a rich and stimulating environment. Consequently, alternative means of expression are of great importance to them. Children express themselves, whether consciously or not, in creative, abstract ways. 'The way we as adults communicate is the tried and tested way, I suppose, not necessarily the natural and only way. As they are yet to learn adult ways, children are more experimental with communication.' An effective early years head should also, therefore, understand children as alternative (and creative) communicators (4.6e).

Stem 4.6	Leaves 4.6a–4.6e

An effective early years leader or manager should...

4.6 Have an approach that advocates creative intelligence	4.6a Promote the holistic development and expression of the creative capacity of children (this involves overcoming the false association of creativity with art and encouraging it as a means of expression)

	4.6b Promote the holistic development and expression of the creative capacity of staff (this involves ensuring that staff build on teaching strengths and that curricula act as scaffolds rather than straitjackets)

	4.6c Promote innovative and individual approaches by staff (this involves encouraging staff to utilize their own idiosyncratic approach to work so that children are more engaged and captivated by their teaching)

	4.6d Understand children as builders and constructors (this involves ensuring that children are encouraged and given adequate opportunity to express themselves (that is, be creative) in a physical capacity)

	4.6e Understand children as alternative communicators (this involves viewing children as experimental communicators who use their creative capacities to explore abstract ways of communicating)

List your targets	
Formulate an action plan	

Reflect on your capabilities and complete the boxes ...

What are your strengths?
Which areas need improvement?
What can you do to build on your strengths?
What do you need to do to improve your skills and
capabilities?

What are your strengths?
Which areas need improvement?
What can you do to build on your strengths?
What do you need to do to improve your skills and
capabilities?

What are your strengths?
Which areas need improvement?
What can you do to build on your strengths?
What do you need to do to improve your skills and
capabilities?

What are your strengths?
Which areas need improvement?
What can you do to build on your strengths?
What do you need to do to improve your skills and
capabilities?

What are your strengths?
Which areas need improvement?
What can you do to build on your strengths?
What do you need to do to improve your skills and
capabilities?

Stem 4.7 Have an approach that advocates emotional intelligence

Cameo: Sandra

Sandra is head of a private nursery. She is not, however, an early years head who 'came from within'. Sandra came into the profession at management level, but as a layperson. She brought with her a wealth of leadership and management experience, including a degree in business management and first-hand managerial experience within the area of human resources. Giving up her job to have children, Sandra returned to work as a nursery head, a job she loves and finds very challenging.

'In my last workplace, the most important thing was to get the job done. But as a nursery head, keeping the atmosphere good and everybody happy and positive is perhaps more important. This is because a good early years service, I think, is the product of a good atmosphere and a devoted team of practitioners. If you concentrate on people – the staff, children and parents – I find that the harmony and support that this brings makes the nursery environment highly conducive to learning and having fun. Children remember when they have fun.'

As she will undoubtedly know, in comparing her previous job to her current one, Sandra has alluded to the two main models in leadership theory: those of 'task leader' and 'relationship leader' (McEwan 2003). Whereas the task leader may be authoritarian and focus on getting the job done, the relationship leader is likely to be democratic and people-oriented, set more in the frame of 'emotional leader' (Hartley 2004).

Needless to say, neither task- nor relationship-leader style is completely effective in isolation of the other, although leadership theorists tend to rate relationship leadership as an ideal style for the 'main leader', with a task leader appointed just below to take care of planning and organizing – the differentiation between leader and manager springs to mind here but also reflects a more team-management approach appropriate in the early years, where different people take on different responsibilities at leader level. Early years providers, however, do not necessarily have the luxury of an extensive leadership or management structure, and so an early years head must combine these two, and many other styles outlined in the Introduction, as and when appropriate. This is known as 'transformational leadership', because the leader transforms the attitudes and beliefs of the staff into a work ethic, creating a shared ethos and philosophy (Daly *et al.* 2004). It places equal emphasis on the process and the people, the product and the service. 'Leadership theory? Oh yes! An effective early years head should be able to adopt a task-leader style when necessary (4.7a) but also be able to adopt a relationship-leader style when necessary (4.7b),' says Sandra. 'Sometimes, it's the only way to survive!'

'I've always believed in using rather than suppressing emotions as a leadership style,' says Sandra. 'The idea that managing with passion and feeling is somehow "anti-intellectual", that human judgement is worse than technical calculation, seems ridiculous to me. I think we all have to manage our emotions and feelings, but we're not computers . . . we can't pretend we don't have feelings and differences . . . and passions.'

Leadership theorists are increasingly supportive of emotional approaches to leadership. Empathy is often mentioned as a vitally important quality because it allows the head to comprehend the feelings of another person and to experience them for oneself. Needless to say, a variety of perspectives are crucial in good early years management. Other leadership qualities or skills often mentioned include the ability to manage frustration and the ability to generate optimism. Emotions and sensitivity certainly have their place in early years leadership. 'Nobody learns a great deal in a sober, efficiency-obsessed environment, neither child nor adult,' says Sandra. Furthermore, early years providers need to have limitless energy; and energy and emotion are often closely connected. In sum, an effective early years head should be aware of the potential of applying, rather than stifling, emotion (4.7c).

In both leadership and educational theory this approach is known as emotional intelligence (Goleman 1996). It is known to comprise four main abilities. The first ability is to be able to identify and isolate emotions in oneself, the second to identify and isolate emotions in others. The third and fourth abilities refer to the necessity of being able to manage these emotions in oneself and in others (see Hartley 2004). Emotions are warranted and enabling, but only if they are controlled and managed. Emotions must be mindful, not mindless (Moyles 2001). An effective early head must have an emotional but stable personal approach to personnel (4.7d). The head must also be able to handle and manage stress – both their own and others'. Stress can be thought of as the wear and tear our bodies experience as we adjust to continually changing circumstances: it has physical and emotional effects on us and can create positive or negative feelings. As a positive influence, stress can help compel us to action and can result in a new awareness and an exciting new perspective on life (4.7e). Too much stress, or badly handled stress, can be damaging to health and to relationships, so it is important to understand how to cope with stress. It is hard to offer advice on coping with stress because everyone – adults and children – copes in their own way. Nevertheless, it is possible to give a few basic guidelines:

- Become aware of the things that stress you – learn to recognize your emotional and physical reactions to stress.
- Recognize what you can change and what you can't change – make a diminishing list starting with the most vital.
- Reduce the intensity of your emotional reactions to stress – talk to someone who can help put the problem into perspective.
- Learn to moderate your physical reactions to stress – slow down, go for a walk . . . whatever helps.
- Build your physical reserves – think about your work/life balance.
- Maintain your emotional reserves – expect some frustrations and be a friend to yourself.

Stem 4.7	Leaves 4.7a–4.7e

An effective early years leader or manager should . . .

4.7 *Have an approach that advocates emotional intelligence*	4.7a *Be able to adopt a task-leader style when necessary (this involves being able to focus solely on a task when necessary and being able to inspire staff so that all pull together to bring the task to its completion)*
	4.7b *Be able to adopt a relationship-leader style when necessary (this involves being able to focus on staff, their needs, weaknesses, strengths and points of view when necessary, perhaps after focusing on a task)*
	4.7c *Be aware of the potential of employing and utilizing, rather than stifling, emotions (this involves overcoming the fallacy that emotion and reason are mutually exclusive and using emotion to good effect rather than suppressing it)*
	4.7d *Have an emotional but stable personal approach to personnel (this involves being empathic, being able to isolate emotions in self and others, and being able to manage those emotions in self and others)*
	4.7e *Understand the reasons for stress and learn to turn stress to one's advantage (this means being able to understand what stresses you and others in the setting and ensuring that 'good' stress is managed and utilized)*

List your targets	
Formulate an action plan	

Reflect on your capabilities and complete the boxes...

What are your strengths?
Which areas need improvement?
What can you do to build on your strengths?
What do you need to do to improve your skills and
capabilities?

What are your strengths?
Which areas need improvement?
What can you do to build on your strengths?
What do you need to do to improve your skills and
capabilities?

What are your strengths?
Which areas need improvement?
What can you do to build on your strengths?
What do you need to do to improve your skills and
capabilities?

What are your strengths?
Which areas need improvement?
What can you do to build on your strengths?
What do you need to do to improve your skills and
capabilities?

What are your strengths?
Which areas need improvement?
What can you do to build on your strengths?
What do you need to do to improve your skills and
capabilities?

Stem 4.8	Leaves 4.8a–4.8e

An effective early years leader or manager should...

4.8 Have an infectious (self-)awareness (continued on next page)	4.8a Be aware of environmental issues and practise eco-friendly procedures and policies (this involves keeping children, staff and parents informed of, and involved in, environmentally friendly practice)
	4.8b Be aware of sex, gender, race, faith and ethical issues (this involves being knowledgeable about anti-oppressive and anti-discriminatory practice and building it into the organizational framework of the setting)
	4.8c Be aware of staff and employment issues, including equal opportunities and other equality issues (this involves having a working knowledge of employment rights of both employer and employee)
	4.8d Have sensitive regard for children, their ethnic backgrounds and their self-concepts (this involves understanding child psychology and development, focusing on the behaviour of the child rather than self)
	4.8e Have sensitive regard for staff, their ethnic backgrounds and their self-concepts (this involves valuing empathy, compassion, openness and encouragement in the workplace, ensuring that staff themselves feel valued)

List your targets	
Formulate an action plan	

Reflect on your capabilities and complete the boxes...

What are your strengths?
Which areas need improvement?
What can you do to build on your strengths?
What do you need to do to improve your skills and
capabilities?

What are your strengths?
Which areas need improvement?
What can you do to build on your strengths?
What do you need to do to improve your skills and
capabilities?

What are your strengths?
Which areas need improvement?
What can you do to build on your strengths?
What do you need to do to improve your skills and
capabilities?

What are your strengths?
Which areas need improvement?
What can you do to build on your strengths?
What do you need to do to improve your skills and
capabilities?

What are your strengths?
Which areas need improvement?
What can you do to build on your strengths?
What do you need to do to improve your skills and
capabilities?

Stem 4.8 (cont.)	Leaves 4.8f–4.8j

An effective early years leader or manager should...

4.8 Have an infectious (self-)awareness (continued from previous page)	*4.8f Have an empathic awareness of the overall needs of children (this involves having a natural as well as an academic understanding of children, drawn from first-hand experience and genuine interest and affection)*
	4.8g Have an empathic awareness of the overall needs of staff (this involves having a generous capacity for empathy and being able to cultivate an environment in which people are valued as individuals as well as team members)
	4.8h Be aware of, and embrace, new technologies and new media (this involves having a positive attitude to technological change, discerning their appropriate use and application, whilst being aware of the impact they have on society)
	4.8i Be aware of equal opportunities and discrimination issues related to sex, age, race, faith and ethnicity (this involves having inclusive policies and ensuring that discrimination is neither tolerated nor fostered in any form in the setting)
	4.8j Be aware of equal opportunities and discrimination issues related to staff, children and parents with special needs (this involves having inclusive policies and ensuring that discrimination is neither tolerated nor fostered in the setting)

List your targets	
Formulate an action plan	

Reflect on your capabilities and complete the boxes...

What are your strengths?
Which areas need improvement?
What can you do to build on your strengths?
What do you need to do to improve your skills and
capabilities?

What are your strengths?
Which areas need improvement?
What can you do to build on your strengths?
What do you need to do to improve your skills and
capabilities?

What are your strengths?
Which areas need improvement?
What can you do to build on your strengths?
What do you need to do to improve your skills and
capabilities?

What are your strengths?
Which areas need improvement?
What can you do to build on your strengths?
What do you need to do to improve your skills and
capabilities?

What are your strengths?
Which areas need improvement?
What can you do to build on your strengths?
What do you need to do to improve your skills and
capabilities?

Stem 4.9 Have a good sense of humour and understand the importance of play and having fun

Cameo: Ayelet

'Although it's not always possible, I try to be as good-humoured as I can. Fun is not something that children alone should be entitled to in the setting. I like to think that my staff have as much fun as the children do. It doesn't matter what type of head you are, things don't always go your way – there are constantly problems to deal with, and you're in continual contact with all types of people. . . . You can't possibly face all this without a sense of humour, without being able to laugh . . . at yourself if nothing else . . . and certainly with the children!'

Ayelet is the head of her local pre-school. Her staff describe her as jovial and easy-going. One member of staff goes so far as to call her 'the resident Victoria Wood', referring to the popular television comedienne. Using humour effectively and appropriately, however, does not comprise telling jokes, making fun and having a permissive attitude to work. It is about creating an environment that is conducive to playing and having fun, where laughter is commonplace, where there is enjoyment in working, playing and being with each other, on the parts of both children and staff. As the culture setter, the head has the most influence on the environment and the atmosphere (see 1.10). An effective head, therefore, should encourage effective and appropriate use of humour in the setting (4.9a).

'Humour is essential when working with children. It can often be incredibly frustrating work, but you can't let this get to you. The rewards far outweigh the difficulties. You have to enjoy it, laugh with them, support them, encourage them to laugh. . . . When children are laughing and enjoying what they're doing, they are far more receptive to learning and develop better dispositions to learning. If you're having fun with them, you have their full attention – it's a stimulus to their concentration.' An effective head will maximize humour as an aid to learning and teaching (4.9b) and understand the relationship that humour and play have with motivation, attention and concentration (4.9c, 4.9d).

The pressures of legislated early years curricula, the ever-increasing focus on learning and child development, not to mention the proliferation of paperwork, all pose a threat to fun and play and people's enjoyment of their work. Whilst the rhetoric of most practitioners is to support play as an appropriate medium for learning and development, this is not always fulfilled in practice, particularly at the level of practitioners' involvement, engagement and interaction in children's play (Bennett *et al.* 1997). This is possibly because some practitioners still do not understand play in any depth and have perhaps not closely observed children at play in such a way as to determine the learning that is taking place.

Although adults distinguish between work and play, children can find both enjoyable and fun. The problem with 'play' is perpetuated by its lack of definition (Moyles 1989, 2005). What is it? We all know intuitively, but describing it in words is incredibly difficult. If the essence of play, however, is fun, enjoyment and choice, then play undoubtedly assists the development of motivation, interest, intrigue, investigation, exploration, independence and concentration. Play does not have to be meaningless, chaotic or noisy (though it may be). Play can be adult-initiated as well as child-initiated, and a balance between these two is always desirable.

It is a fallacy that, with age, play and fun should decrease. The phrase 'work and play' reflects adults' priorities. Of course, adults have to 'work' to make money, but work does not have to exist in isolation to play. How many of us regularly work at our play and, indeed, play at our work? Adults often seem to draw the distinction between work and play but this does not mean that children have to. Play is known to be a facilitator to learning and cognitive development (Bruce 2004). Staff and parents are also entitled to their share of fun and play.

The experienced curriculum should ideally be play based (as emphasized in many policy and curriculum documents at both local and national level). 'Active learning', as opposed to 'formal learning', is perhaps a better way of conceptualizing play. An effective head should sponsor play-based learning and curricula (4.9d) and understand the role of play in cultivating the investigative and experiential nature of children's learning and development (4.9e).

Self-discipline, self-motivation and self-restraint are all very important and need cultivating through play, too. Children will all too quickly make their own distinctions between play and work. It is up to the head to balance these two reconcilable opposites. An effective head will also cultivate an environment where children learn an appropriate degree of moderation and self-restraint (4.9f).

'Strange as it may sound, play is not something that comes easily to all children,' says Ayelet. Her claim brings to attention another important point about fun and play. Children have different levels of confidence. Some children are shy and reserved, others are confident and self-assured. It is up to the head to ensure that staff assist all children to gain the most educational and social benefits from their play. Social competence is also discernible through play because it is, more often than not, a social activity (see Broadhead 2003). Through it, the level of confidence and social competence of a child can be diagnosed and developed. An effective head will understand play as an important social activity in which some children and some adults will need some help in which to engage and interact (4.9g).

Stem 4.9	Leaves 4.9a–4.9e

An effective early years leader or manager should...

4.9 Have a good sense of humour and understand the importance of play and having fun (continued on next page)	4.9a Promote effective and appropriate use of humour in the setting (this involves creating an environment that is fun rather than comedic, in which fun is used positively, creatively and non-oppressively)
	4.9b Maximize humour as an aid to learning and teaching (this involves ensuring that children are having fun whilst learning, as well as understanding how humour can be used to engage the attention and memory of children)
	4.9c Understand the relationship humour has with motivation, attention and concentration (this may involve gauging the degree of humour appropriate to the setting and devising curricular activities that are fun)
	4.9d Understand the relationship play has with motivation, attention and concentration and promote learning through a play-based curriculum (this involves looking beyond the false dichotomy of work and play and instead conceptualizing play as an important activity that is meaningful and therapeutic)
	4.9e Understand the role of play in cultivating the investigative and first-hand experiences of children (this involves encouraging children to be both independent and interdependent)

List your targets	
Formulate an action plan	

Reflect on your capabilities and complete the boxes . . .

What are your strengths?
Which areas need improvement?
What can you do to build on your strengths?
What do you need to do to improve your skills and
capabilities?

What are your strengths?
Which areas need improvement?
What can you do to build on your strengths?
What do you need to do to improve your skills and
capabilities?

What are your strengths?
Which areas need improvement?
What can you do to build on your strengths?
What do you need to do to improve your skills and
capabilities?

What are your strengths?
Which areas need improvement?
What can you do to build on your strengths?
What do you need to do to improve your skills and
capabilities?

What are your strengths?
Which areas need improvement?
What can you do to build on your strengths?
What do you need to do to improve your skills and
capabilities?

Stem 4.9 (cont.)	**Leaves 4.9f–4.9g**

An effective early years leader or manager should . . .

4.9 Have a good sense of humour and understand the importance of play and having fun (continued from previous page)	4.9f Cultivate an environment where children learn moderation and restraint (this involves maximizing the power of play to develop morals and ethics, as well as to cultivate social skills such as sharing and communication)	

	4.9g Understand play as an important social and cognitive activity in which some children (and adults) require support to engage and interact (this involves having an appreciation of the different levels of comfort people feel towards play and humour)	

List your targets	
Formulate an action plan	

Reflect on your capabilities and complete the boxes ...

What are your strengths?
Which areas need improvement?
What can you do to build on your strengths?
What do you need to do to improve your skills and capabilities?

What are your strengths?
Which areas need improvement?
What can you do to build on your strengths?
What do you need to do to improve your skills and capabilities?

Use this space for writing

Use this space for writing

Use this space for writing

7 Using ELMS – drawing it all together

Introduction

The ELMS tree has been extensively explored in the previous chapters. ELMS, as we have seen, tries to tell what actually happens in leadership rather than discussing the issues around leadership (Mitchell 1990). In this final chapter, we first look at the uses and benefits it has before moving on to a few final thoughts about the issues surrounding early years leadership and management.

Purposes, uses and benefits of the ELMS tree

The obvious use of ELMS is as a self- and peer evaluation tool for early years heads. There are many other potential uses of the tree. For example, when the project began, the main uses of the final document were foreseen by the researchers as being for:

- quality assurance purposes;
- peer evaluation;
- making organizational changes to the setting;
- evaluation of the general running of the setting;
- identifying areas of necessary professional development for the head and senior staff;
- auditing and managing leadership training;
- general organizational purposes.

To these our focus group added:

- pre-inspection evaluation of leadership and management aspects;
- head of setting mentoring support (i.e. either two heads working together in support of each other, or one head receiving support from a local authority designated mentor);
- information for the management group;
- senior staff evaluation (i.e. those likely to become leaders/managers);
- additional support and information for leadership and management courses such as NPQICL;
- uses for the purpose of employing a new head (i.e. information about the qualities, skills, attributes, characteristics and attitudes required of an excellent leader and manager).

Users will no doubt think of other purposes for the document and its outcomes which meet their particular circumstances. This is fine: there need be no restriction (or lack of imagination) in the way the ELMS tree is perceived or the purposes for which it is used.

As with the NPQICL, ELMS offers a number of additional benefits to those undertaking evaluation. It 'builds on participants' own experiences to extend their understanding of learning about leadership' and it 'provides a deeper understanding of the skills needed to lead and manage a children's centre' (National College for School Leadership/Pen Green Centre 2005: 3). It also means that the head can take the initiative in her/his own professional development using ELMS to identify and locate various components of the role and undertake thoughtful examination and exploration of strengths, challenges and weaknesses. Similarly, we welcome people adding to our typology – something like this is never finished, but always evolving, just like the head's role in leading and managing an early years setting. Jillian Rodd has recently suggested (2006: 5) the field of early childhood 'does not have a commonly accepted definition of leadership, nor has it engaged in a systematic debate about the properties of . . . leaders'. We fervently hope that this book will inspire such debate and also encourage more research by and with practitioners in an attempt to find some of the answers to the many areas requiring development.

It is sad to note that early years practitioners, including heads, still seem, as Rodd says, 'reluctant to regard themselves as intellectuals with a responsibility and capacity for scientific enquiry' (2006: 199). In doing so, practitioners are perpetuating the perception that they are 'lower-status' workers – the practitioners in Moyles and Adams' study (2001) were far more concerned initially with practice than with theory, although extended opportunities for professional and personal development and reflection soon had them all working as researchers. Undertaking research and engaging with that of others can be a valuable tool for change, and there is no doubt that change is going to be the order of the day for many years to come in the early childhood field. Instead of using personal and professional 'ideals' as the basis of practice, it is vital that heads, especially, promote and engage with research knowledge both external and internal so that they can influence local and national policies. It is far easier and more effective to question policy makers from a position of knowledge than from one of intuition.

As we saw in the Introduction, despite leadership (as a concept) featuring prominently in the past 10–15 years, it seems that issues such as legislated curriculum and target setting may put leaders once gain in the 'management' realm, that is, in ensuring accountability to those imposing the restrictions. This is contrary to the modern concepts of leadership embraced within ELMS where the leader uses a social democratic approach to motivating and inspiring staff in an atmosphere of collegiality rather than hierarchy. As Fullan (2003: 22) suggests: 'When so many demands are placed on the principalship, it is not just the sheer amount of work that is the problem, but it is also the inconsistent and ambiguous messages. Take control but follow central directions; make improvements, but run a smooth ship and so on.' Early years heads need to be sufficiently confident in their own knowledge and in their ability to evaluate new initiatives that they can adopt and adapt what is good to meet the needs of the children and staff in the setting. For too long, early years practitioners have lacked a full political voice: with the backing of exemplary heads, the time has now come to make our views on effective early years practices clear to policy makers. Successful leaders do not learn how to 'do' leadership and then 'stick to set patterns and ways of doing things along a prescribed set of known rules. They are willing to change in response to new sets of circumstances – and to the differing needs of children, young people and teachers – and they are often rule breakers' (Riley and MacBeath 2003: 174).

The Chinese philosopher Lao-tzu, the founder of Taoism, wrote: 'The journey of a thousand miles begins with a single step.' Lest it seems to early years head that they have a long journey ahead of them in relation to evaluating and enhancing their vital role as settings' leaders and managers using ELMS, let us reiterate that many heads are well on the way to becoming exemplary heads and they should use ELMS as a way of celebrating their skills and knowledge. For it is known that 'successful leaders have breadth and emotional maturity; they are more shock-proof than other people and are neither over-elated by success nor crushed by failure' (O'Sullivan 2003: 6). Leaders present a 'dynamic perspective to their followers: not just a headline or snapshot, but a drama that unfolds over time, in which they – leaders and followers – are the principal characters or heroes. Together they have embarked on a journey in pursuit of certain goals, and along the way and into the future, they can expect to encounter certain obstacles or resistances that must be overcome' (Gardner and Laskin 1996: 14).

Good luck and good judgement to all our users on their particular leadership journey.

References

Adams, S. (2005) Practitioners and play: reflecting in a different way. In J. Moyles (ed.) *The Excellence of Play*. Maidenhead: Open University Press.

Adams, S., Alexander, E., Drummond, M.J. and Moyles, J. (2004) *Inside the Foundation Stage: Recreating the Reception Year*. London: Association of Teachers and Lecturers.

Aubrey, C., Harris, A., Briggs, M. and Muijs, D. (2005) *How Do They Manage: An Investigation of Early Childhood Leadership*. TACTYC Conference, November 2005. Presentation supported by ESRC grant RES-000–22–1121.

Baker, C. (2001) *Foundations of Bilingual Education and Bilingualism*, **3rd edn. Clevedon: Multilingual Matters. In many settings, partnership with the wider community means dealing with issues of languages of different ethnic groups. This well-conceived book is a vital read for heads working with families and communities for whom English is a second or additional language.**

Bartholomew, L. (1996) Working in a team. In S. Robson and S. Smedley (eds) *Education and Early Childhood*. **London: David Fulton. This is a short but informative chapter about leading a team and the importance of cultivating a team ethic and culture, with additional sections on change management, leadership qualities and working in partnership with parents.**

Beetlestone, F. (1999) *Creative Children: Imaginative Teaching*. Buckingham: Open University Press.

Bell, L. (2002) 'Strategic planning and school management', *Journal of Educational Administration*, 40(5): 407–24.

Bennett, N., Wood, E. and Rogers, S. (1997) *Teaching through Play: Teachers' Thinking and Classroom Practice*. Buckingham: Open University Press.

Bennett, N., Crawford, M. and Cartwright, M. (eds) (2003) *Effective Educational Leadership*. London: Paul Chapman/Sage/The Open University.

Broadhead, P. (2003) *Early Years Play and Learning: Developing Social Skills and Co-operation*. London: RoutledgeFalmer.

Brooker, L. (2002) *Starting School: Young Children Learning Culture*. **Buckingham: Open University Press. Young children have to 'acculturate' themselves to different environments at a very early age. This book explores how they 'learn the rules' and the effects upon children of transitions from pre-school settings to schools.**

Bruce, T. (2004) *Developing Learning in Early Childhood*. London: Paul Chapman/Sage.

Caldwell, B. (2003) Foreword. In M. Ebbeck and M. Waninganayake (2002) *Early Childhood Professionals: Leading Today and Tomorrow*. Sydney, Australia: McLennan & Petty.

Collins, J. (2001) *Good to Great*. New York: HarperCollins.

Crawford, M. (2003) Inventive management and wise leadership. In N. Bennett, M. Crawford and M. Cartwright (eds) *Effective Educational Leadership*. London: Paul Chapman/Sage/The Open University.

Daly, M., Byers, E. and Taylor, W. (2004) *Early Years Management in Practice: A Handbook for Early Years Managers*. **London: Heinemann. This is an up-to-date, practical handbook written specifically for students of early years management. It covers all the recent issues and is suitable for a wide range of courses. The books include case studies taken from the early childhood field and the theory is clearly placed in this context throughout. The accessible, jargon-free style is tailored to the needs of the practitioner, making this an essential handbook.**

Day, C. (2004) The passion of successful leadership, *School Leadership and Management*, 24(4): 425–37.

Day, C. (2005) *A Passion for Teaching*. London: Routledge. This is a fascinating theoretical book with practical examples which highlight the various forms of intellectual, physical, emotional and passionate endeavours in which teachers at their best engage. Day demonstrates that having a passion for teaching has been identified by researchers as one of four main leadership characteristics. Passionate practitioners believe they can make a difference – to learners and to learning and teaching.

DfES (2004a) *The Children Act 2004*. London: HMSO.

DfES (2004b) Green Paper, *Every Child Matters*. Nottingham: DfES Publications.

Drury, R., Miller, L. and Cambell, R. (2000) *Looking at Early Years Education and Care*. London: David Fulton. This book explores some of the basic underlying issues which managers and practitioners alike must take account of in their own settings to promote effective practices.

Duffy, B. (2004) Creativity matters. In L. Abbott and A. Langston (eds) *Birth to Three Matters: Supporting the Framework of Effective Practice*. Maidenhead: Open University Press.

Ebbeck, M. and Waninganayake, M. (2002) *Early Childhood Professionals: Leading Today and Tomorrow*. Sydney, Australia: McLennan & Petty.

Edwards, C., Gandini, L. and Forman, G. (eds) (1998) *The Hundred Languages of Children: The Reggio Emilia Approach – Advanced Reflections*. London: Ablex.

Fabian, H. and Dunlop, A-W. (2002) (eds) *Transitions in the Early Years: Debating Continuity and Progression for Children in Early Education*. London: RoutledgeFalmer.

Fatt, J.P.T. (2000) Charismatic leadership, *Equal Opportunities International*, 19(8): 24–8.

Fink, D. (2005) *Leadership for Mortals: Developing and Sustaining Leaders of Learning*. London: Paul Chapman.

Fullan, M. (2001) *Leading in a Culture of Change*. San Francisco, CA: Jossey-Bass.

Fullan, M. (2003) *The Moral Imperative of School Leadership*. Thousand Oaks, CA: Corwin, and London: Sage.

Gardner, H. and Laskin, E. (1996) *Leading Minds: An Anatomy of Leadership*. New York: Basic Books.

Ghaye, A. and Ghaye, K. (1998) *Teaching and Learning through Critical Reflective Practice*. London: David Fulton.

Gold, A. and Evans, J. (1998) *Reflecting on School Management*. London: Falmer Press.

Goleman, D. (1996) *Emotional Intelligence: Why It Can Matter More Than IQ*. London: Bloomsbury.

Goodfellow, J. (2000) Knowing from the inside: reflective conversations with and through the narratives on once co-operating teachers, *Reflective Practice*, 1(1): 25–41.

Grace, G. (1995) *School Leadership*. London: Falmer Press.

Guild, D., Lyons, L. and Whiley, J. (1998) Te Whaariki: New Zealand guidelines for an early childhood curriculum, *International Journal of Early Childhood*, 30(1): 65–70.

Handy, C. (1989) *The Age of Unreason*. New York: Random House.

Harris, A. and Lambert, L. (2003) *Building Leadership Capacity for School Improvement*. Maidenhead: Open University Press.

Hartley, D. (2004) Management, leadership and the emotional order of the school, *Journal of Education Policy*, 19(5): 583–94.

Hatano, G. (1995) Conceptual Change: A bridging notion between cognitive development and instructional research. Paper presented at the European Conference on Learning and Instruction. Nijmegen, The Netherlands.

Heifetz, R. and Linsky, M. (2002) *Leadership on the Line: Staying Alive through the Dangers of Leading*. Boston: Harvard Business School Press.

Horner, M. (2003) Leadership theory reviewed. In N. Bennett, M. Crawford and M. Cartwright (eds) *Effective Educational Leadership*. London: Paul Chapman/Sage/The Open University.

Hunt, K. and Robson, M. (1999) Empowering parents of preschool children, *International Journal for the Advancement of Counselling*, 21(1): 43–54.

Isles-Buck, E. and Newstead, S. (2003) *Essential Skills for Managers of Child-centred Settings*. London: David Fulton. Focusing on how managers should behave in order to ensure that they and their team members are providing an excellent service to all children in their care, this book provides a balance of accessible theory and practical application for a wide range of settings. It offers step-by-step guidance on: becoming a manager; linking theory to practice; developing personal skills in managing people and services; and becoming more confident and effective.

Jackson, D. (2003) Foreword. In A. Harris and L. Lambert, *Building Leadership Capacity for School Improvement*. Maidenhead: Open University Press.

Johnson, J. (1999) *Improving Personal Effectiveness for Managers in Schools*. Stafford: Network Educational Press.

Kydd, L., Anderson, L. and Newton, W. (eds) (2003) *Leading People and Teams in Education*. London: Paul Chapman/The Open University.

Law, S. and Glover, D. (2000) *Educational Leadership and Learning: Practice, Policy and Research*. Buckingham: Open University Press.

Lipman-Blumen, J. (1992) Connective leadership: female leadership styles in the 21st century workplace: sociological perspectives. Pacific Sociological Association. Available at http://www.achieveingstyles.com/article_female.asp. Accessed 1 March 2006.

Lyus, Verna. (1998) *Management in the Early Years*. London: Hodder & Stoughton. A text for higher level childcare qualifications which include a management component. This covers the range of management functions (planning and leading); skills (interpersonal and diagnostic); and roles (for example friend, colleague, teacher). There are useful sections which explore vision, planning and mission statements. Within the chapter on management models is a section on leadership, introducing all of the main theories and theorists.

Mailhos, M. (1999) Reflective practice and the development of pedagogical reasoning, *Pedagogy, Culture and Society*, 7: 329–58.

Maslow, A. (1943) A theory of human motivation, *Psychological Review*, 50: 370–96.

McEwan, E. (2003) *Seven Steps to Effective Instructional Leadership*. Thousand Oaks, CA: Corwin.

Mintzberg, H. (2004) *Managers not MBAs: A Hard Look at the Soft Practice of Managing and Management Development*. San Francisco, CA: Barrett-Koehler.

Mitchell, J. (1990) *Revisioning Educational Leadership: A Phenomenological Approach*. New York: Bergin & Garvey.

Moyles, J. (1989) *Just Playing? The Role and Status of Play in Early Childhood*. Buckingham: Open University Press.

Moyles, J. (2001) Passion, paradox and professionalism in early years education, *Early Years*, 21(2): 81–95.

Moyles, J. (2005) *The Excellence of Play*, 3rd edn. Maidenhead: Open University Press.

Moyles, J. and Adams, S. (2001) *StEPs: Statements of Entitlement to Play*. Maidenhead: Open University Press.

Moyles, J. and Musgrove, A. (2003) *EEPES (EY) Essex Effective Pedagogy Evaluation Scheme (Early Years)*. Chelmsford, APU/Essex County Council.

Moyles, J. and Suschitzky, S. (1996) *Jills of All Trades . . .? Classroom Assistants in KS1*. Leicester/London: University of Leicester and Association of Teachers and Lecturers.

Moyles, J., Adams, S. and Musgrove, A. (2002) *SPEEL: Study of Pedagogical Effectiveness in Early Learning*, Report No. 363. London: DfES. This study reports on a Framework for Effective Pedagogy with 129 components of effectiveness against which practitioners' skills and knowledge can be evaluated. Useful for all managers for staff appraisal.

Muijs, D. and David, R. (2001) *Effective Teaching: Evidence and Practice*. London: Paul Chapman.

Muijs, D., Aubrey, C., Harris, A. and Briggs, M. (2004) How do they manage? A review of the research on leadership in early childhood, *Journal of Early Childhood Research*, 2(2): 157–69.

Murray, L. (2002) Public relations and communication management, *Journal of Communication Management*, 7(1): 9.

National College for School Leadership/Pen Green Centre (2005) NPQICL information. Available at http://www.ncsl.org.uk/aboutus/pressreleases/college-pr-24052004.cfm?jHighlights=NP-QICL. Accessed 1 March 2006.

Nivala, V. and Hujala, E. (2002) *Leadership in Early Childhood Education*. University of Oulu, Finland.

O'Sullivan, J. (2003) *Manager's Handbook (Early Years Training and Management)*. Leamington Spa: Scholastic Publications.

Oldroyd, D., Elsner, D. and Poster, C. (1996) *Educational Management Today: A Concise Dictionary and Guide*. London: Paul Chapman.

Paul, J., Costley, D.L., Howell, J.P. and Dorfman, P.W. (2002) The mutability of charisma in leadership research, *Management Decision*, 40(2): 192–200.

Reynolds, M. (1999) Standards and professional practice, *British Journal of Educational Studies*, 47(3): 247–66.

Riley, K. and MacBeath, J. (2003) Effective leaders and effective schools. In N. Bennett, M. Crawford and M. Cartwright (eds) *Effective Educational Leadership*. London: Paul Chapman/Sage/The Open University.

Robson, S. and Smedley, S. (eds) (1996) *Education and Early Childhood: First Things First*. London: David Fulton.

Rodd, J. (1998) *Leadership in Early Childhood*, 2nd edn. Buckingham: Open University Press.

Rodd, J. (2006) *Leadership in Early Childhood*, 3rd edn. Maidenhead: Open University Press. This book is an excellent resource for early childhood practitioners who want to understand how to create successful childcare and early education settings and how to lead and manage them. This third edition has been fully revised and reflects important changes affecting leaders in early childhood: increasing flexibility required of children's services, working in multi-disciplinary teams, and an increasing emphasis on the importance of early education. This edition also includes new case studies and examples based on an extensive international study of early childhood leaders and is a must for all early childhood leaders and managers.

Sadek, E. and Sadek, J. (2004) *Good Practice in Nursery Management*. Cheltenham: Nelson Thornes.

Shakeshaft, C. (1989) *Women in Educational Administration*. Newbury Park, CA: Corwin.

Sharp, P. (2002) *Nurturing Emotional Literacy*. London: David Fulton.

Shulman, L. (1999) Knowledge and teaching: foundations of the new reform. In J. Leach and B. Moon (eds) *Learners and Pedagogy*. London: Paul Chapman/The Open University.

Siraj-Blatchford, I. and Clarke, P. (2000) *Supporting Identify, Diversity and Language in the Early Years*. Buckingham: Open University Press.

Smith, A. and Langston, A. (1999) *Managing Staff in Early Years Settings*. London: Routledge. This book draws on a wide range of management theory and shows its relevance and relationship to early years settings. Case studies are used to provide the starting point for reflection, and throughout the chapters readers are asked to consider the examples, stand back, interpret and audit their own actions in order to develop their management skills. This book will assist managers and prospective managers by providing them with the tools to facilitate staff training sessions or to conduct personal enquiry into the working of their own organization.

Solley, K. (2003) What do early childhood leaders do to maintain and enhance the significance of the early years? Paper presented at the Institute of Education, University of London, 22 May.

Steinberg, S. and Kincheloe, J. (1998) *Students as Researchers – Creating Classrooms that Matter.* London: Falmer Press.

Sylva, K., Melhuish, E.C., Sammons, P., Siraj-Blatchford, I. and Taggart, B. (2004) *The Effective Provision of Pre-School Education (EPPE) Project, Technical Paper 12, The Final Report: Effective Pre-School Education.* London: DfES/Institute of Education, University of London.

Taggart, B., Sylva, K., Siraj-Blatchford, I., Melhuish, E.C., Sammons, P. and Walker-Hall, J. (2000) *The Effective Provision of Pre-School Education (EPPE) Project, Technical Paper 5, Characteristics of the Centres in the EPPE Sample: Interviews.* London: DfEE/Institute of Education, University of London.

Whalley, M. (1999) Women as leaders in early childhood settings – a dialogue in the 1990s. Unpublished PhD thesis, University of Wolverhampton.

Yorke-Barr, J. (2001) *Reflective Practice to Improve Schools.* London: Sage.

INDEX